"Enough good, clean, old-fash[...]
Day and his entire family tree [...]
—[...]

"A hilarious one man/woman show that reminds us of the importance of discovering that one moment where it all makes sense to you."
—John Scoles, *Winnipeg Sun*

"Hip, glib, and clever. What makes us care is the awesome communicative abilities of the writer/performer. Intelligent, witty, in control of his material and his audience, Hagen's commanding performance is what powers this *Edmonton Queen*."
—Colin MacLean, *Edmonton Sun*

"Fascinating and funny; a unique and important slice of prairie history."
—*Vue Weekly*

"Performed with verve and sincerity. Hagen delights in admitting he's the boy your mama warned you about."
—Chauncey Featherstone, *Vue Weekly*

"Be careful, guys. Some of these stories are intriguing enough to make you take a quick glance through your sister's closet."
—Don MacArthur, *SEE Magazine*

"An amusing and raucous ride through an Edmonton you never knew existed . . . a sort of Priscilla of the Prairies."
—Richard Cairney, *SEE Magazine*

"Eloquent, exuberant and, at times, uncomfortably frank."
—David Crosson, *Outlooks Magazine*

"Hagen has the gift of gab. And he tells a bizarre, humane story in extravagant, mock heroic, hothouse language that seems as right as red lipstick for the occasion. Unmissable."
—Liz Nicholls, *Edmonton Journal*

The Edmonton Queen
The Final Voyage

For Stephanie - - -

Darrin Hagen

BRINDLE
& GLASS

For licensing agreements or more information about any of
Darrin Hagen's plays please email kevin@guysindisguise.com.
For more information about Guys in Disguise go to www.guysindisguise.com

Library and Archives Canada Cataloguing in Publication
Hagen, Darrin, 1964–

Edmonton queen : the final voyage / Darrin Hagen.
Originally publ. under title: The Edmonton queen, not a riverboat story.

ISBN 1-897142-20-X

1. Hagen, Darrin, 1964-. 2. Transvestites—Alberta—Edmonton—Biography.
3. Female impersonators—Alberta—Edmonton—Biography. I. Title.
HQ76.98.H34A3 2007   792.702'8   C2006-906595-0

Front cover photo: Peter McClure © 1993
Back cover photo: Ian Jackson
Cover deign: jellyfish design, www.jellyfishdesign.com
Author photo: Charles McDuff Gillis
All photos from the interior courtesy of the author, except for those listed on page 247.
Every effort has been made to credit the photos appropriately. Please contact the author or
the publisher with any omission or error. It will be rectified in a furture printing.

The author wishes to thank the Edmonton Arts Council
for their contribution to this project.

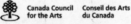

Canada Council   Conseil des Arts
for the Arts   du Canada

Brindle & Glass is pleased to thank the Canada Council for the Arts and the
Alberta Foundation for the Arts for their contributions to our publishing program.

Brindle & Glass is committed to protecting the environment and to the responsible use of
natural resources. This book is printed on 100% post-consumer recycled and ancient-forest-
friendly paper. For more information, please visit www.oldgrowthfree.com.

Brindle & Glass Publishing
www.brindleandglass.com

1 2 3 4 5 10 09 08 07

PRINTED AND BOUND IN CANADA

For Lulu . . .

Sometime in every lifetime, you meet a person who changes your perception.

This story is dedicated to the queens who lived it, but none of it would have happened quite the way it did were it not for the boundless enthusiasm, unlimited imagination, and frightening creative streak of Charles McDuff Gillis.

Through his eyes the world was a much more intense experience, and my world became a richer, more exciting place.

These stories are his as much as mine; the mythologies sprang from his brow in a Niagara-like torrent as the rest of us struggled to keep up. The Family he created was one we all desperately needed, and one by which we were all nourished. Lonely, shy young men from all over Canada found a way to belong; under his wing, we discovered our worth.

We discovered ourselves.

The language, terminology, humour and mythology that make up this book were authored not by one person, but by many who, through an accident of geography, shared one experience.

All I had to do was remember it. Like I could ever forget.

. . . with love, Gloria
1997

"HERE I AM.
IN EDMONTON, ALBERTA.
WHAT A DUMP!"
*Christopher Peterson impersonating Shirley MacLaine
channelling Bette Davis
on JuJu Dogface's Psychic Alliance
"TVTV: Transvestite Television"
Guys in Disguise, Edmonton International Fringe Festival 1995*

Table of Contents

Gloria ❧ 1

Somewhere in a field near Tofield ❧ 7

A River Runs Through It ❧ 9

Lulu ❧ 15

Flashback (Not The Literary Device) ❧ 19

Creation ❧ 29

One Man's Garbage . . . ❧ 39

Forgo the Fabulous and Embrace Anarchy ❧ 43

It Happened One Halloween ❧ 53

In The Beginning ❧ 57

A Legend In Her Own Lunchtime ❧ 61

Giving Birth Is A Messy Experience ❧ 69

Armageddon ❧ 81

Two Men Enter—One Man Leave ❧ 89

Little House On The Prairie ❧ 95

Go Into The Light ❧ 107

Boys Will Be Girls ❧ 113

Heavy Is The Wig That Wears The Crown ❧ 123

She Stoops To Conquer ❧ 125

All That Glitters . . . ❧ 133

Cry Me A River ❧ 141

A Fish Out Of Water ❧ 145

The Truth About Fried Eggs ❧ 153

I'll Be Seeing You . . . ❧ 157

The Queen's English (A Lip Glossary) ❧ 169

The Imperial Houses Under Millicent ❧ 176

The Gospel According to The Hole Family ❧ 182

The Queen Is Born ❧ 183

Flashback ❧ 189

The Bigger Picture ❧ 199

Final Voyage ❧ 211

The Queens Have Their Say ❧ 221

Gloria Broadcasts Her Thanks ❧ 246

Photo Credits ❧ 247

About the Author ❧ 248

Gloria, 1983.

Gloria

GLORIA COMES OFFSTAGE PANTING. She struts on her seven-inch stilettos into the dressing room, tosses her jewellry onto the counter and heaves her seven-foot frame into a chair in front of the mirror. Her eyes lock with the reflection of her eyes, heavy and dark, oversized lashes dragging the lids down like a pair of cement pumps. Someone told her once they looked sultry.

She had believed them.

The hair is a giant puff of blond tendrils, piled yet falling, done yet undone. Wide enough on the sides to draw attention away from her so-square shoulders. Ruby plum lips. Beauty mark always here. It's the last thing on and usually the first thing off. But she's not done for the night, so it stays.

Two performances have taken their toll on her makeup. The sweat runs through her eyebrows, collecting in an oil slick under her eyes.

It's the closest she's ever come to looking like a football player.

She crosses her legs and surveys the damage. Phyllis Diller would have an easier job.

She pulls a breast out of her bra and pats her forehead dry. The pancake peels off like cheap paint, forcing her real skin out of hiding. She wails in despair. Fixing a face can take longer than building one from scratch.

And it's only twenty minutes until . . .

Fame. Adulation. The gig of the century.

If someone phoned you and asked if you wanted to go-go dance at the base of the city hall clock tower with a spotlight creating a shadow of your gyrating frame four storeys high on

New Year's Eve at the stroke of midnight in front of a hundred thousand people—

You wouldn't consider whether or not it was a good idea to be outside in go-go wear in a minus-forty-not-including-wind-chill climate;

You wouldn't consider whether or not it was a good idea to be dressed like that at an alcohol-free-family-food-fun-fireworks-type spectacle;

You would say yes. Immediately. Gloria did.

And now she's faced with emergency facial maintenance, a costume change, packing up her clothes and costumes and transporting them from the Library Theatre across Sir Winston Churchill Square to City Hall at twenty minutes to midnight through tens of thousands of people. In the winter. In heels. Without an assistant.

Gloria was never big on logistics.

Praying silently, she panic powders. A white haze expands around her head as she puffs copious amounts of talcum. Soon she is as pale as Glenn Close in *Dangerous Liaisons*. And just as bitchy. But the black keeps bleeding through like a haunted paint job in a B movie.

Okay, don't panic. Plan B.

When all else fails, cover up.

Take out all the pins in the wig. Pull the hair around the face. Tell people you saw it in *Vogue*. Necessity is the dragmother of fashion intervention.

Gloria slips out of her universal "little black dress." *(Author's note: this term is not a literal but a figurative one. A little black dress on Gloria could contain enough fabric to slipcover a hearse).*

She pulls out her one-piece Star Trek jumpsuit with the Tit-to-Toe red stripe down the side, chosen because at least most of her skin will be covered, albeit in some bargain synthetic. She quickly inflates two medium-sized balloons, leaving lipstick all over the mouthpieces, and places them in their appropriate positions, where they are held in place through the miracle of stretch poly blends.

Then, in horror, her eyes travel down her front where she sees . . .

The Bulge.

The bane of every queen's existence. The ultimate giveaway. The line separating the men from the broads. The equipment. The boy toy.

In her haste, Gloria had forgotten to pack her dance belt.

The Star Trek jumpsuit with the Tit-to-Toe red stripe is, in a word, form-fitting. It greedily hugs every square millimetre of Gloria's larger-than-life frame. Hardly appropriate for a family gathering. You couldn't even get away with that at a fag bar. Now, without going into gory detail about what a queen does with the equipment while in drag, understand that it can be extremely distracting.

Gloria begins throwing clothes around the room, searching frantically for any solution—a wrap, a scarf, a belt. Nothing. Then her eyes land on the blue feather boa.

Tonight's obviously going to be about improvising.

The boa, wrapped around her hips at crotch level, looks ridiculous. She's beginning to resemble a sci-fi ostrich. But there's just not enough time to come up with anything else.

Outside, on street level, the square is in full winter bloom. Lights. Music. People. Colour. Costumes. Presiding over the whole thing is the city hall clock tower. It reads 11:45.

Gloria has now packed up everything into a frenzy of 7-Eleven bags, hangers and a battered hockey bag. She has made a decision that the fastest way to city hall is underground. Through the subway tunnel. She bursts into the tunnel, then regrets it immediately as the door safety locks behind her.

The tunnel is harshly lit, throbbing with noise and packed with people as far as you can see. It's the pre-midnight buzz— anticipation and bliss and relief and nostalgia all supercharged with an annual intensity. Children in tinsel masks, adults with balloon helmets, all heading to the fireworks.

Gloria endures the snickers, sneers, the "O my God"s, the kids' rude questions as she tries to jog through the insanity, her heels clicking loudly on the tile, inflated breasts heaving, the boa around her bottom emphasizing the graceless gait of a giant. Sparks fly on every second step from the missing cap on her right spike; she comes on like some obscene cartoon superheroine on her way to save the planet.

With only minutes remaining.

It's the longest block in her lifetime.

Finally, she arrives at her post. She looks up and her jaw drops.

Somehow, in her head, she had always pictured a gilded go-go cage to cavort in.

Somehow, in her head, she had imagined being surrounded by people delighted at her antics and cheering her on.

Somehow, in her head, she had always pictured it looking more like an episode of Solid Gold.

What she had not imagined was a makeshift plywood platform four feet square, shaky, with nine rickety steps hastily nailed together. Hundreds of yards from the action in the centre of the square.

Life can be so cruel.

The clock tower reads 11:51.

Unsteady, she climbs the steps to her post. The platform is small, wobbly and covered in a thin sheet of glare ice. No railing. She turns and sees her silhouette—gigantic, shivering, unsteady, with bad poodle-type hair that moves in the wind like a nest of snakes.

The cold starts to sink in. She begins to dance just to keep warm, but there's not a lot she can manage on the tiny platform. And there's another problem: in minus forty weather, balloons tend to shrink. Now the balloons stay in place in the jumpsuit as long as they are large. But the compressed cold air means a difference of about ten bra sizes. Now they shift around as if they're being driven by a remote control in the hands of an insane driving instructor.

Hardly the look she was striving for.

Wearying of her humongous shadow, she turns to look at

the square, and that's when it happens.

She stares directly into the million watt searchlight. Everything else disappears. Her retinas singe and sizzle, and immediately, temporary blindness sets in. She takes a step too far back and plunges out of sight with a short surprised scream and lands in a crumpled heap in a snowbank.

The clock tower says 11:54. She had danced for exactly three minutes.

Now she limps with one broken high heel, bags in tow, like a crazy bag lady caught in a parade, struggling through the crowd. One breast has wiggled its way toward her shoulder, while its partner has slipped to belt level. Frost has formed on her sultry lashes, making blinking a stiff, crunchy affair. Slipping and lurching, she makes her way through the alley, only to find herself stuck in a dead end. Of course, everything's locked. She can't get through.

The clock tower says 11:59.

The countdown.

At the stroke of midnight, with fireworks going off and people hugging and singing a block away, Gloria falls to her knees and starts to cry. A balloon pops and it starts to snow.

The Hole Family Thanksgiving.

FlashQuack.

Somewhere in a field near Tofield,

sometime near the end of the twentieth century,
on a farm far, far away . . .

. . . THERE MAY STILL STAND AN ABANDONED OUTHOUSE, white paint peeling, door flapping in the wind, the wooden seats long deprived of the touch of moons.

If it still stood, which it may, you could look inside, and it would take a moment to realize that the tiny marks covering the walls are not bugs or dirt but, in fact, writing: dense, confusing writing in Jiffy marker covering all three walls and the inside of the door.

If you could find the beginning of the saga, it would tell you . . .

First there was Dorkness, then there was Light.
Then there was Bud Light . . .

You would read on to learn of the creation of Bimbolimbus Slug Destruction, conceived in a flash of cosmic coincidence, who spawned a zillion stars.

Of course, it's all in code.

But a translator could show you that it is, in fact, ancient proof that a mighty family was born in these wilds. The outhouse walls speak as loudly and eloquently as any Rosetta Stone, preserving forever the moment near the end of the millennium when lunacy met inspiration and gave life to a new spirit.

Thus a family was born.

Or at least that's one theory.

Graduations, 1982.

A River Runs Through It

July, 1982

ONCE UPON A TIME . . .

Isn't that how all fairy tales start?

The Greyhound bus leaves Rocky Mountain House twice a day: 7:00 AM and suppertime. Not being a morning person, my ticket was for the latter. That way I could say goodbye to Mom, pack my clothes and my accordion, and go watch the North Saskatchewan for a while.

When you stand on a bridge, an illusion occurs. Watching the water slide silently past you in July, the first thing that occurs to you is how clean the water is. A brilliant aquamarine blue that I've never seen anywhere else. The water flowing underneath makes it feel like the whole bridge is moving backward. Suddenly I'm Barbra Streisand on the boat in "Funny Girl" holding that impossible long note.

In Rocky Mountain House you don't tell people you listen to Barbra Streisand.

I took my journal, some school papers, and the love letter from an older man in Edmonton that almost got me thrown out of the house.

An older man. He was thirty-three. I'm thirty-three. I'm hardly an older man.

I stood on the bridge, ripped them to pieces, and watched them spin and flutter down to the water, where they gradually disappeared into the brilliant clear blue.

I wondered how long it would take to float to Edmonton. If only I had a boat. I knew where I would end up. I had already been there once.

Flashback.

This is not a riverboat story. It's my story. Actually, it's their story.

It's our story. The Lucky Ones.

The Greyhound stops at Alhambra, Leslieville, Benalto, Eckville, Sylvan Lake and Red Deer.

Keegstra Country. (Jim Keegstra, a high school teacher in Eckville, was charged with teaching his students that the Holocaust never actually happened. The case received national coverage. Eckville is just north of Caroline, where the Aryan Nations have a lovely farm.)

I could have gotten there faster on the river. I could have *floated* into town.

But back then I was a little more subtle.

At Red Deer, Calgary and Edmonton are exactly the same distance away. Why North? Would things be different if I had turned South?

Probably not. Besides, the river runs North.

And it's my river.

FLASHBACK.

Every once in a while, a queen is born. Whether through osmosis or immaculate misconception is still mostly a mystery, but they appear. Suddenly and without warning, a new pretender to the throne stands in front of you. Under the terms of the Sisterhood of Unrecognized Royalty, they all get their grab at the tiara at some point in their career.

But where do they come from? Genderfuck meteors flaming to earth? Cross-dressers crawling from every crevice in the country? Often, they mutate out of men from the most macho of environments. But what triggers it?

For many, the transition is as swift as it is brutal and final. And it happens once a year.

A night where nothing is really what it seems, when pretty boys become susceptible to suggestion, when reality moves aside and dreams take over, when vision is diluted by bright lights, acid trips, and masks.

Every year, on October 31, thousands of Alberta men cross the line on the one night when they are actually permitted to do so. They cross the line that was drawn in the sandbox in front of them at the age of two. The line that shapes their thinking, their manner, their insecurities, their stress, their careers, their lives, their perception.

They cross that line and for one night, they know.

They put on a dress.

And every year, some of these men don't return.

Because once they're on the other side, the world looks different. And they get hooked. Big time.

The drug of attention, adoration, disgust, applause, glamour, ego, applause, political incorrectness, applause, applause, applause, did I mention applause?

Whether it's because the real world is so drab and hopeless, or because there are too many shackles, or because somebody said "no" one too many times, or because you're too femme to fit, or because it makes your cock hard, or just because you're

Gloria, 1987.

Neon, Gloria, Iris and Lulu, 1987.

too fabulously dramatic, and stylish for your own good.

You try it.

You love it.

You buy it.

Not just the outfit. The lifestyle.

There is a moment of illumin-ation that very first time, when you finish painting the face. You reach for the wig, slip it on, and your eyes lock with your eyes in the mirror.

For a moment, everything else disappears.

You see someone looking back, a total stranger that you recognize immediately.

You see your sister, your alter ego, the only woman that will ever understand you. A combination of your mother, the wife you'll never have, the woman you'll never be.

Your eyes lock with your eyes, and a destiny you never pictured locks into place.

You fall in love. With the woman in you.

And the man you thought you were will do anything to make her dreams come true.

It can happen to anyone.

These stories are true. Mostly.

The really bizarre stuff is true.

Actually it's all true.

All I had to do was remember. Like I could forget.

None of the names have been changed, because there are no innocents, but occasionally the outfits I describe are nicer than what they were actually wearing.

It's beyond difficult putting these times and people into perspective. Back then, we had no perspective. The drugs were cheap, and we were beautiful. Or was that the other way around?

There was only the next show, the next party, the next hit, the next john, the next pageant, the next Barbra Streisand album.

The eighties sashayed past us in a crinoline haze, a cloud of dreaming bigger than anyone should. Foam and fur and feathers and false lashes. It was like living backstage with the Muppets, only they were more realistic.

Delusions of Grandeur dressed by Value Village.

Our enormous visions. These tiny gowns.

Lulu, 1983.

Lulu

Sometime in 1982
The Strip: Downtown Edmonton

LULU STANDS ON THE CORNER of boredom and desperation, her fried Diana Ross wig illuminated by the blinking hotel lights. Pink Yellow Pink Yellow Pink.

Big girl. Built like a Soviet hockey player, but with better fashion sense.

She stands there: all mood, all rude, all attitude.

The cars circle 'round and 'round the square, the headlights tracing a thick bright circle around her and she bends down to look in the windows and some cars slow down and some speed up and each get a wink or a finger and some come 'round again and some give up. But not the Caddy.

Ahhh, the Caddy. Built for comfort. Like her. Lots of legroom. She's a big girl. And she's in heels. And has been for hours.

The Caddy. If she could get in she could rest her size 14B puppies. Her blisters yelp as she struts the sidewalk pretending it doesn't hurt but it does and she leans on the parking meter and wishes she worked at a Mr. Submarine. They make you wear a hairnet, but you get to wear flats.

Ahh, the Caddy. Maximum headroom. Good for big hair. She's a big girl. She wears big hair well.

The Caddy circles like a silver shark, testing the water for motion. Lulu sucks in her waist to appear more willowy. She drags on her Camel, bends down and gives him a look that says, among other things, that if he slammed on his brakes right here, right now, she would be his bend-over baby doll for the night. It's a look dripping with enough innuendo to fuel every car that didn't pick her up tonight. That's a lot of juice.

The window opens a crack. Through it she can smell the

bucks. Lulu can smell a rich Daddy better than a sow hunting for truffles. It's a heady combo of cigar smoke, anticipation and tinny top forty that envelops her senses. In his glasses, she can see the reflected tail lights of cruising station wagons, sedans on the hunt.

From where he sits, the split ends of her fried Diana Ross wig look like a halo flashing Pink Yellow Pink Yellow Pink.

From where he sits, the safety pins don't show, and the rise and fall of her balloons as she sucks on her Camel make him whimper under his breath.

From where he sits, she's a goddess, floating in a diaphanous fog of exhaust and steam and smoke, swooping down to his car, a heavenly vision of sexual release, an Angel all in black.

He's been drinking.

He looks out the window, sees a sweet young thing. Humpin' on the parking meter, leanin' on the parking meter, oh she looks so good.

The Caddy swims up to the curb. Lulu steps up to the Caddy. The parking meter heaves a sigh of relief. She leans over and coos through the crack, "Wanna play, Daddy?"

As she waits, she shifts the pain in her feet from left to right to left. Anticipation mounts. At this point in her workday, she would suck him off for free just to be able to sit down for ten minutes.

The door clicks open. Lulu folds herself into the passenger seat with the grace of a pro, hair not even touching the roof. She slips off her pumps and rubs her toes together in the heat.

"Seventy bucks and it's yours, Daddy."

But Daddy's not listening. His eyes are glued to her feet. He watches the toes wiggle around under the sheer mesh of four pairs of Shoppers Drug Mart pantyhose. He's wondering if she'll think he's a total pervo because all he really wants is those toes in his mouth.

Lulu sees Daddy eyeing her feet and panic punches her stomach around, because her feet are always a dead giveaway— and this makes her nervous 'cause oddly enough some men get turned off by finding a penis on the woman they're renting so to change the subject she says: "You can't fuck me tonight 'cause I'm on the rag, but I give a blow job that'll make your head cave in."

As he pulls the Caddy back into the stream of headlights he purrs, "How about a foot massage?"

Lulu can't believe her bead-encrusted ears. The big hair goddesses were beaming love on her tonight!

They pull into a parking lot littered with used condoms and spent fantasies. Money changes hands, her feet land in his lap and in seconds she's transported into reflexology heaven. He's good.

She moans and gasps, not because that's what she does but because that's what she gets paid to do.

From where he sits, the stubble growing through her thick pancake makeup is merely a halo kissing her cheek.

From where he sits, the oversized special edition lashes, one of which went on a little crooked, are light and wispy like feathers.

From where he sits, the one gradually deflating breast merely adds an asymmetrical loveliness.

He's drunker than he thought.

Suddenly, the night is alive with red and blue and searchlight white and it's a bust and Lulu freaks because of that silly repeat offender thingy and she makes a break for it.

She falls out of the car and runs for her life, crashing through the underbrush like a bull moose bellowing for freedom. The official insults hurled at her merely bounce off her back. She hits the sidewalk and runs like a girl down the street, arms pumping, purse swinging viciously, balloons heaving from the effort. The Diana Ross wig flies off her head and lands under the wheels of a passing garbage truck. She glances over her shoulder pad to find—no one in pursuit. Running like a girl slows to walking like one. She's free.

And her feet feel fabulous. Daddy knew his stuff.

It is then that she looks down and realizes her size 14B black

Lulu heads out.

patent leather come-fuck-me pumps with Joan Crawford ankle straps are still in the Caddy, with Daddy.

She made seventy bucks. New shoes are $97.50.

Back at the Caddy, the cops deal with the john.

The only clue to the girl that got away is a pair of 14B black patent leather come-fuck-me pumps with Joan Crawford ankle straps. Somewhere out there is a hooker big enough to fill those shoes.

There's a reward. Enough to buy a lot of shoes. But she's too embarrassed to collect.

The next night, she's back on her corner.

Flashback

(Not The Literary Device)
1976–1990

EVEN A BLACK HOLE CAN HAVE A personality. In a world without rules, there is still tradition. And etiquette. When you pull out of society, you still need a place to hang out. With friends.

You wanna go where everybody knows you're gay.

Far from the surface of The Big Onion, in an obscure corner of downtown, a four-story red brick building leftover from the warehouse era was Home to thousands.

Every weekend its inhabitants would toss off soiree after bash after debauched shindig. To be invited, you merely had to be well dressed, superbly coiffed, famous, infamous, filthy rich, devastatingly beautiful, near-naked, encased in plastic, dripping in chains, balanced on spikes that could kill, a fabulous dancer, an exhibitionist, a voyeur, a swinger, a drug dealer, sleeping with the deejay, a go-go speaker boy, a muscle boy, a pretty boy, a boy, a model, a punk rocker, a jock, a dyke, a fag, a fag hag, a drag hag, straight, bi, celibate, sexy, aloof, brooding, mysterious, scary, extreme, tireless . . .

Well, you could be almost anyone, really. But even then, you had to be prepared to wait in a line stretching as far as The Foxy Lady Disco Dancing Lounge for an hour or more. And name-drop your way through the front door.

Unless you were a Queen.

If you were a Queen, you could show up whenever your nail polish finally dried, unfold yourself from your taxi, and waltz in the front door of the Club, past the lineups of commoners, knowing that they were all envious of the ease of entry, the familiarity of fame, the drama. Of Drag.

It was a world where *we* wrote the rule book.

It was *us* they came to see: the Stars of the Underground.

And we never disappointed.

Monday to Friday was spent planning, sewing, trying on, colour draping and stockpiling narcotics. Even if you weren't planning to crank, dressing up was a major event. We had reputations to uphold. As freaks, we *were* the show. It was our responsibility to be bigger than life, and we took that challenge seriously.

The plebeians depended on us.

Our schedule was strict, the itinerary regimented:

FRIDAY:

2:00 PM: Awake.

4:00 PM: Awake again. Get up.

4:30 PM: Remove last night's makeup.

5:30 PM: Put on makeup to cover makeup that won't come off. Go buy cigarettes.

6:30 PM: Count the acid. Plan the dose.

7:30 PM: Awake. The cigarette has burned a hole in the couch.

8:30 PM: Remove makeup. Shave. Moisturize. Begin applying Night Makeup.

10:30 PM: Face completed. Search drag room for anything to wear.

"Lulu, what are you wearing tonight?"

"You can't wear my palazzo pants."

"As if I would."

"I'm doing the shimmy-fringe number."

"With or without the vinyl purse?"

"Without."

"I left my purse at the Club . . . can I—"

"Fine. Just don't lose it."

"Why can't I wear your palazzo pants?"

"Because they would look like a slipcover on you."

"Yeah . . . but they match the purse."

Find Lulu's shimmy-fringe for her. Secretly pick out the silver lamé palazzo pants for yourself.

11:00 PM: Accessorize. It's the only thing that separates us from the lower animals. Lulu always used to say that jewellery should be worn in multiples of seven.

11:30 PM: Light a joint. Call a cab. Take the first hit of acid.

11:35 PM: Last minute costume change. Palazzo pants are so retro . . . decide instead on the standard rich hooker ensemble. But this needs the black patent Joan Crawford come-fuck-me pumps, which are buried in the attic. Start to dig. Lulu begins to reconsider the whole genderfuck punk goddess motif, and starts eyeing the silver lamé palazzo pants. She tries them on.

11:45 PM: Cab arrives. You don't hear him honking 'cause you and Lulu are fighting over the silver beaded purse.

11:50 PM: Emerge from the house wearing Lulu's punk goddess motif, she in the silver lamé palazzo pants. Fold yourself into the taxi: Careful! The hair! The bigger the hair, the closer to God.

Midnight: ARRIVE! Step out of the cab, adjust your skirt to hide the run in your nylons, scream with joy, look down your nose at the poor hetero commoners in the line up, breeze past

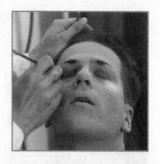

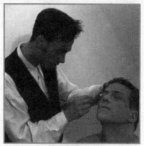

Kim Burly makes Gloria beautiful.

Twiggy makes Gloria beautiful.

them, say hi to the Reverend Brother Bob, push through the crowd, dump your furs in the office, sneak up behind a bartender and grab his ass. "Freepour me a Scotty—don't bruise the ice like you did me last time. Don't you look sassy? Boyfriend out of town again? Make it a quadruple and I won't tell him a thing. Where are The Girls standing? Oh, stop looking, I found them." Strut through the crowd, receive compliments. "Fuck, who let all the straight chicks in, it's like a Mary K graduation. They all dance the same: boing, boing, turn around, boing, boing, turn around—oh my god I love this song! Let's dance. Who's got the poppers? No, up here, I want everyone to see this outfit. Get off the speaker, bitch, we live here! Isn't that the Razzberries? God, where did all these Barry T's wannabes come from? It's like a Barbie convention only hideous. Donna Summer is so fabulous, isn't she? I know we're supposed to hate her now but the MUSIC!"

12:45 AM: Meet in the ladies' can at the pre-arranged time, in the handicapped cubicle. Squeeze everyone in. Sit on the floor, screaming with laughter at absolutely anything. Drop the acid. Pass around the hairspray. Stay until some dyke kicks you all out for reinforcing negative stereotypes of women. Leave in a huff.

1:00 AM: Get that feeling in your stomach that lets you know your drugs are working. "Another Scotty . . . Queen size, please." Lulu's drinking beer out of a bottle with a long straw so she doesn't mess up her lipstick. Sit high on the bar, your legs crossed so you can torment straight boys. Watch the dance floor like it's a campfire, flickering and flashing and undulating and hypnotizing. Cheer as two guys in muscle shirts climb on a speaker and start tearing off each other's clothes. The Club is full, and the beautiful people keep pouring through the door. Some guy can't take his eyes off your tits so take one out and pat his forehead dry.

1:15 AM: Hallucinate. Lulu's talking about something, screaming in your ear. Nod and pretend you can understand her. The guy is now licking your legs. You feel too sorry for him to tell him that you can't feel a thing because you're wearing four pairs of Shoppers Drug Mart pantyhose.

1:30 AM: Ditch the guy. Find The Girls.

1:45 AM: Grab Lulu and head to the walk-in beer cooler. Take off your shoes and stand on the cold steel until the swelling in your feet goes down. Once shoes fit again, renew dancing.

2:00 AM: Last call. Ignore it. You know management.

2:30 AM: Whine to management for more scotch. Hang out with the bartenders while they count their tips. Make so much noise they kick you out. Leave in a huff.

3:00 AM: Start looking for a party. If unsuccessful, reconvene in the handicapped stall and start your own.

3:30 AM: Hang out in the kitchen, even though the lighting is brutal. Laugh as Gretchen passes out. Last song is playing, and hundreds of party animals start lining up for their coats. Get more scotch.

4:00 AM: Decide against calling a cab. You and Lulu have

decided, in your stoned wisdom, to walk home. Head down Jasper Avenue, still in heels, arm in arm, the morning sun revealing the stubble growing through the all-night makeup. A van starts circling the block. Then it pulls up beside you. The side door slides open and there's five guys watching you. You cross the street, hoping they'll go away. The van turns and pulls alongside you again. You cross again, and this pisses them off. They pour out of the van and run toward you. Lulu rips her stilettos off her feet. "Weapons, girl!" I do likewise. We swing our heels at men we've never met, hoping it's all a sick joke, but they want blood. Lulu gives it to them. Her stiletto connects with a forehead and blood streams out into his eyes. "C'mon, fuckers, you're not gonna let a couple of queens take you out, are ya?" taunts Lulu, as we dodge blows and swing pumps and scream like warriors. When they run off, wounded, realize how lucky you are to be alive. Realize how lucky you are to be Lulu's friend.

4:30 AM: Go into the Mac's store and call a cab, even though you only live a block away. The guy working behind the counter watched the whole thing, and never called the police. Buy cigarettes and wait in the store for the cab. The guy asks if we would please wait outside. We ask if he would please fuck off. Leave in a huff.

5:00 AM: Go to bed. Have trouble sleeping. You're not sure if it's from the acid, or the uppers, or the black eye. Avoid thinking about your life.

SATURDAY: Rinse. Repeat.

FOR FIFTEEN YEARS, Flashback remained the Guardian of everything that was avant, cutting edge, or alternative. People didn't get hired, they transmogrified until they belonged. Then they started getting paid. Like a huge talent magnet, it attracted outcasts and thrill-seekers.

If you knew you belonged, you stayed. There was room for many on the ride; over the years, thousands of queens and fags and leather boys and future celebs passed through its hallowed doors. Lulu and I were both there when Wayne Gretzky showed up *after* last call and demanded champagne. His then girlfriend, Vicki Moss, was wearing a fake fur (long before it was politically correct to do so). Disco star Sylvester watched a bad drag show one night; Sarah McLachlan partied in the office with us while we cashed out; Belinda Carlisle danced all night to Go-Go's tunes; The Nylons wore Lulu's Empress campaign buttons home; Craig Russell let us treat him like the Godmother of all drag; The Jazz Butchers drank like kings; the drummer from Heart pissed off Kim Burly and was removed from behind the bar (she had no idea who he was, even though we had just seen the concert the night before); Mrs. Lougheed tried to check her fur coat during a fashion show, and when she couldn't, the coat check girl was fired, causing more gossip column fodder; the Speaker of the Legislative Assembly came in once, and all night we made jokes about dancing on the speaker; Scott Thompson of The Kids in the Hall talked about himself even more than

Gloria and Cleo strike a pose, 1988.

*Twiggy on stage
at Flashback.*

I did; Long John Baldry would lean on the bar and check out which pretty boy he liked best (a thrill's a thrill); k.d. lang showed up when her name still contained capital letters; Kurt Browning did a pirouette at the main bar (we wouldn't serve him until he did); Mark Messier dragged his brother in, only to prop him up all night (he drank too many Oralyzers); the Ghermezians tried to butt in line, and Lulu told them they weren't well dressed enough and sent them away; Steve Anthony of Much Music was pretty full of himself for a dwarf; the lead singer of Twisted Sister sent someone to the Club to find him a date, so we hooked him up with Tiffany, our most stunning cross-dresser; Divine called every time she was in town, looking for marijuana; and any time there was a touring musical or dance show or rodeo finals or large-scale figure skating event in town, the dance floor would be packed with new temporary faces, amazed that you could find a location that decadent on the prairies, amazed that a New York-style disco could exist in the Provinces.

If this is the circus, sign me up and point me to the bearded lady. Life in the Fab lane. All you had to do was live through it.

Home. This was where Family could take root, be fruitful, and multiply.

Home.

Lulu and Gloria's first show, and first public photo shoot, 1983.

Lulu.

Creation

Halloween 1982

FLASHBACK. SECONDS AFTER WITNESSING my first drag show, I began the search for my dragmother. I was one of the Lucky Ones. I was adopted immediately. Without a mother figure to take you under her hemline you would merely float on the fringe, looking for a way into the scene. Outsiders themselves, queens are by nature suspicious of outsiders.

Your dragmother became your mentor, model, motivator and finally your main competition if things progressed naturally. Once she had taught you all the tricks in her arsenal, it was in your job description to dethrone her. In the natural scheme of things, there can only be *one* queen. Like a beehive of court intrigue, the battle to the death was both public and passionate.

One night I saw my drag twin. Immediately, I asked the bartender what her name was.

Lulu LaRude.

When I first met her, it became immediately obvious that we were of the same mould. Both of us were tall, impossibly loud, wild, and had size fourteen shoes. Like gigantic screaming Barbie dolls with no "off" button. Instantly the scale shifted. With another giant beside you, you don't feel so freakishly tall. Often we were mistaken for each other, in and out of drag. She hadn't been around long, in fact she was fresh off the street (literally), but she took me in like a pro, and together we began terrorizing any show we could bully our way into.

She partied with a queen aptly named Trash. The two of them were wild women, creating looks and characters from the refuse of garage sales, back alleys and hardware stores. The night I first laid eyes on them, they were making a one-time-

Trash answering the iron, 1982.

only appearance as Chandelerious and Vivvy Pink. Neo-Punk Valley girls decorated with extension chords. Trash (as Vivvy) was wearing a plastic neon striped tablecloth stolen from Earl's, and carried a clear plastic purse filled with live grasshoppers. Lulu's Chandelerious was a camp, drugged out Connie Francis-type creation with a blond hairpiece perched on her head, teased a good seven inches high. Her '50s party dress was shredded, burnt and stained, and held together with staples and safety pins. They floated through Flashback on a Quaalude cloud, connected by cables and chords, outcasts from the Glamour circuit, living a fashion anarchy.

They were like me.

Only free.

I looked at Lulu and knew I had found her. Lulu LaRude became my dragmother.

We fucked, because that's how you met people back then.

In a sacred ceremony, we did a midnight dip in the giant fountain, visited Purple City, lit a joint off the eternal flame in front of the Legislature, and Trash and Lulu anointed me with the name that would immortalize me underground for eternity. I held my breath, probably because I had just had a toke, and waited for The Name.

"I dub thee: Gloria Hole," Lulu said majestically, touching each shoulder with the Rhinestone Turkey Baster.

"What??" Not quite what I had pictured.

"Trash thought of it. Isn't it fabulous?"

"It's you. It's fabulous!" added Trash.

"But I was kinda hoping for something more . . . dignified."

Lulu laughed. "Get over yourself, honey. Dignity is something you earn. You have so much to learn."

"You know, we could just go back to calling you Naomi Fuckstick."

"No! No . . . Gloria's fine, I guess . . . but—Hole?"

Lulu took a deep hit off the joint. "Mark my words, Gloria. The Hole family name will be a mighty one in this town someday."

For the next four years, we spent every minute of every day together. Like family.

Lulu loved life on the edge. It was where she did her best work.

I would watch her putting on her makeup, trying to make sense of the many phases of faces. We drank Southern Comfort (very Janis Joplin) and listened to Midler and would head to the bar, or I would drop her off on the Strip by the Holiday Inn and wait for her at the bar, where she would tell tales of perverts and freaks, laughing about the fights she sometimes had to get into. One of her favourite lines once she had the trick's money was "By the way, I'm a queen. I hope you don't mind."

Most of them didn't. Men usually don't.

Her sense of humor had a mean streak. When I was fighting with my psychotic fag hag roommate one day, Lulu suddenly jumped into the argument. "Gloria, it's her birthday. Don't be mean to Shirley." I was about to shoot back something mean

Lulu and Neon, on the 10th anniversary of Lulu's reign as Empress.

when I saw a glint in her eye. So I sat and watched as Lulu won Shirley over. "Let me do your makeup for your birthday dinner. It'll be my present to you." I watched as Lulu painted the heaviest whore face I've ever witnessed, keeping a straight face as she cooed over Shirley's "classic bone structure." Shirley left for her date, the door closed behind her, and Lulu burst out laughing. "She didn't even look in the mirror!" she howled.

I realized how lucky I was that she was my friend.

Eventually we got thrown out of that apartment. Lulu moved in with Ricky and I started camping on Deejay's couch. Deejay was a Satanist. I slept in her altar, surrounded by black candles, black velvet paintings of the devil, and books on black magic. Lulu was never far away, though, and when the witch stuff started to freak me out, Lulu and I moved into a house together with Annie Hole and Joolz, two diametrically opposed women who worked at Flashback.

The one thing we all had in common was a bad attitude toward the world. We were antisocialites. Joining us on occasion were members of a Cowtown gang: Flora Tron, Guy, Ty Morgan, and a larger-than-life queen trapped in a woman's body named Sister Neon. As long as the drugs flowed, we were happy; strolling through our neighbourhood connected by chains, draped in leopard print, mohawks pointing angrily to the sky. Annie supervised the proceedings, the reincarnation of Nina Hagen, her black lips sucking on a Virginia Slim while she cued up the vinyl. We liked our music loud and annoying.

We frightened people.

Lulu and Gloria, 1983. The Dragon Queens' first photo shoot.

We weren't drag queens; we were Dragon Queens. Separately, Lulu and I were manageable; together, never.

We made a pact: we would be next. Together, we could rule this town. The Big Onion was ours for the taking.

Well, almost.

This game was ruled by tradition. Like any age-old ritual, it had rules and etiquette. Crowns garnered respect.

We had to be crowned to make it official.

Not an easy task; Lulu needed to get off the street and get a real job (hooker didn't look good on the application form for Empress) and I hadn't even done my first drag show yet. But everyone around me knew it was only a matter of time.

They knew a queen when they saw one.

So night after night, I danced on the speakers, performing every song that got played. When my first big break came, it wasn't from Lulu. She was still pretty much an outsider. I was asked by the reigning Empress, Mrs. K., to perform in the next show. Only one stipulation: I had to do it in black drag.

Before the politically correct amongst you fly off the handle, let me explain: most of the world's best drag music is sung by black women. We relived the lives of these tormented divas through their amazing music: pumps planted on the stage, gospel-inspired vocals tearing through our souls . . . it remains, to this day, the best lip-synching material around. So for us to do a whole show in black drag was the biggest gift we could give back to these ladies who had given us so much. Not to mention it was a lot of work, and black panstick was expensive. Also, realize that I'm not talking about Al Jolsen with white lips and gloves to match. If there was one thing these queens knew, it was their makeup technique.

I sat in a chair in the drag room, looking at the creation in the mirror.

Lindee Star had done an amazing job. A tall, beautiful, Amazon goddess looked back with my own eyes. (*Author's note: photographic evidence does not verify this claim.*) I watched her closely, discovering her facial expressions, examining her from every angle, like recognizing a total stranger. I was terrified to go onstage. She, however, had been ready all her life.

I remember my knees shaking as I stood in my new slingbacks. I remember the music: "It's Raining Men" by The Weather Girls. I remember thinking that nothing would be the same after this moment.

I remember how lucky I felt. I remember . . .

. . . the Applause.

AT THE PARTY afterwards I saw the way the past monarchs were treated. With respect.

Crowns garnered respect.

Around this time, a strip agent that we partied with offered us our first professional gig. She wanted to start booking drag acts in lieu of the strippers that she usually sent to bars. Even though my drag career was less than a week old, Lulu and I said yes and started to put together a show.

"If you're gonna do this, we might as well go buy you some real tits," she said. I had "borrowed" hers for my debut, but we were both in this show, so we needed two sets. We went to the bra department at Woodward's and searched for a saleslady. After standing around being ignored for fifteen minutes, we approached an older, non-threatening, matronly woman.

"Can you show us where your prosthetic breasts are?" asked Lulu, as if it were the most natural thing in the world. The saleslady didn't bat an eye. "Certainly," she said, efficiently, and led us to the back of the department. She went to a set of small drawers set discreetly into the wall, opened one, took out a decorator box, opened it and removed a velvet bag with a drawstring, opened it and took out something wrapped in bubble plastic. She unwrapped the plastic, and proudly displayed the breast.

"It's only four hundred and fifty dollars. Top of the line."

Lulu and I looked at each other, trying not to laugh. The saleslady was only trying to be helpful, but she had clearly misunderstood.

Lulu smiled and, without missing a beat, said, "Have you got anything in foam?"

We were very practical girls, in many ways.

A WEEK LATER, we stood on a tavern stage in front of a grimly silent bunch of straight farmers in Gibbons, Alberta, population 2,335. They had all showed up looking for naked female flesh, and were instead presented with two six foot eight amateur drag queens lip-synching to a loud ghetto blaster. When one of the drunker patrons began screaming he wanted to see some tits, Lulu pulled out her foamies and threw them onto his table. "Here, you can hold onto these. Now shut your hole, honey, 'cause mine's making money." The audience howled. The heckler even laughed. It was my first experience with the power of shock, of turning the tables and making your freak status into a weapon. It seemed life on the street had prepared Lulu for anything . . . especially dealing with hostile men. Gradually the mood shifted from hostility to mild amusement, and by the end of the show, they were even clapping. We each made fifty bucks. It was the first time I got paid for doing drag. On the way home, I said, "Oh my god, that was tragic. What are we going to tell everyone?"

Lulu looked at me like I had just asked to stupidest question in the world. "We tell them it was fabulous." We got to the Club and boasted of our triumph, and suddenly we were professional Queens.

Perception is nine tenths of reality.

Now that Lulu had a source of income (I had also gotten her a job at Flashback), and we were approaching legitimate queenliness, we decided we needed a crown. Each. This wasn't just us being greedy—there were several crowns up for grabs. Just pick one and go for it.

Lulu decided to run for Empress. Her campaign image was "Tootsie." Lulu would arrive in a smart, businessy power skirt, complete with sensible red hair and glasses. I was her campaign manager. We were nineteen.

She lost to an Old Guard Dowager, Mary Mess.

Tradition stated that the Runner-Up would always be appointed the title of second-in-line to the throne: Lulu became the eighth Imperial Princess.

But not before the first Empress chewed her out for wearing jeans to a campaign show, the second Empress and I got in a fist fight, while Empresses three through seven just generally scowled their disapproval. They were not amused.

Lulu and I didn't do traditional drag. We took our cue from Trash, who had risen from the genderfuck depths to become Mz. Flashback on little more than pure imagination. Crowds adored her even though she had never donned an evening gown.

She was our inspiration.

Trash, 1983.

One Man's Garbage . . .

1983

WHAT WE THROW OUT DEFINES US; what we leave behind, even more so.

Trash had been a nomad from an early age, as long as anyone could remember. She floated into town an unknown and was soon a regular fixture on the Hill, where tough boys and pretty boys and Indian boys merged to party, scrap, buy, and sell. Sixteen going on a thousand in experience; young but frighteningly wise.

She spent her life casting off the things life collects as you live it. Refusing to be tied down by conventions of home, she moved often, shedding furniture and drag, leaving stuff in alleys and apartments.

Trash was one of our primary influences. Bravado to the *nth* degree, dressing out of Hardware as much as Women's Wear. Drag was an intensely public experience for Trash, whose motto was "It's not worth doing if you can't freak out some straight boys." So on Halloween, rather than doing a show in the bar, she would crank it up loud and head to Victor's (a swanky downtown eatery), and drink free scotch from drunk businessmen horny enough to be confused by her trollopy . . . well, Trashy presence. She was public enough that gossip columnists often commented on her presence at events like Klondike Days, where she scandalized the midway, or reported her legendary battles with her Mr. Flashback. We all read it in the news when Trash resigned her title because she wasn't cast as Marilyn in the Dead Celebrities Halloween show.

She hung the crown in a 7-Eleven bag on the apartment doorknob of Bianca Bang-Bang, who *was* playing Marilyn, and

Bianca Bang-Bang, who was playing Marilyn—this was the first drag show I ever saw.

headed out for the night in drag.

And did her own show.

Somewhere.

Living randomly, as Trash did, turned the city streets into a canvas. Not content to perform onstage, she took her unique brand of anti-fashion out for strolls. While there, she could furnish her life from the discarded treasures of civilians. Her dwelling was always an experience unto itself: found couches, scavenged lamps, coffee tables made of shards of broken mirror balanced on cement chunks and railway ties. As Trash was only five seven, it was often a mystery as to how she actually transported some of these monoliths back to home base, but she wasn't the type to let something as trivial as physics keep her from decorating her world.

She was the first Live Art I had ever met.

ONE DAY LULU and I sat on a low brick wall, watching the endlessly boring K-Days parade schlep past. It was about to rain, as it always did, and we were bored, as we usually were. A discordant marching band shuffled past, clutching their sheet music as a huge gust of wind threatened to scatter the melodies across the sky. Lulu and I passed a joint back and forth, giggling about how funny straight people were when they tried to stage a big event. The most glamorous thing we had seen so far was the Klondike Kate convertible and, frankly, we had better fashion sense. Lulu laughed. "It looks like Laura Ingalls in a toilet-paper cozy!"

Suddenly a scream was heard from three blocks away. Not a

scream of fear or warning as much as a scream of announcement, of arrival. Everyone around us looked in the direction of the scream. There, walking toward us, in a drugged out crinoline cloud, feathers in her hair, dress cut down to there, a banner across her foamies that read "Klondike Queen," tossing Flashback swizzlesticks at the children, was Trash.

Lulu and I screamed with laughter, then shouted to her. She heard, looked over to us with a glint in her eye, and joined us on the wall. Together, we laughed at the parade, laughed at people staring at us, laughed as Trash filled us in on her afternoon's exploits.

"I did a hit of acid and decided it was a good day for a parade. I didn't even know there was already one happening! So I just joined in." She started bragging about the boys she had been tormenting as she trolloped through her afternoon. It was always kind of hard to believe that any guy would be fooled by someone dressed like she was, but as I sat there, disbelieving, Lulu shushed both of us and said, "Jocks in convertibles: three o'clock."

"Chomp," we all agreed under our breath.

A moment of reverent silence as the beefcake float drove closer. They were Oilers or Eskimos or something butch like that, I've never been able to tell them apart. Just as they pulled past us, Trash screamed "Hi, honey! Give a girl a lift?"

The Jocks all looked in her direction and waved, then one of them motioned for her to get in.

"That's my cue, see ya later!" She jumped off the low wall, navigated through a bunch of kids, then trotted as fast as she could manage in those heels after the motorcade, as Lulu and I sat silent, our jaws hanging wide open.

The jock's face changed expression gradually as Trash drew closer. Remember, distance is a girl's best friend. She probably looked fairly alluring from across the street, but up-close drag reality in daylight is a sobering thing.

No one can blend *that* well.

By the time the jock figured out what he was dealing with, it was too late. Trash had climbed into the convertible and sat high on the back, waving like the perfect pageant winner. Short of physically tossing her onto the asphalt, there wasn't a lot he could do. The last thing he needed was a photo of him roughing up what looked like a woman, albeit a garishly dressed one.

As they drove away, we saw Trash put her gloved hand on the jock's knee. He did nothing; just sat, staring straight ahead as his buddies howled with laughter.

Lulu and I sat in awe. "Go, girl," we whispered admiringly. Silently, we saluted, giving the Royal Wave: hat-2-3, purse-2-3, pearls-2-3, wave and rest.

Trash pauses with Lulu before terrorizing a professional sports team at the K-Days Parade.

Forgo the Fabulous
and Embrace Anarchy
1984–1985

LULU AND I SHOPPED AT VALUE VILLAGE, had weird hair and would wear anything:

Garbage bags and rhinestones.

Plastic wrap with high heels.

I specialized in lampshade hats with hairpieces flowing out of them, and vintage cat-eye glasses. Waitress uniforms.

Lulu was a little sleazier: catsuits and mohawks, sink plugs for earrings.

There was a touch of road warrior in everything we did.

We decided that our route to fame was a simple one: just be the weirdest people in the world and the world would be our oyster. We'd stroll down Jasper Avenue, singing "Cry Me A River" in full throttle falsetto, ignoring the stares from passers-by. It was our favourite song. We'd get on a bus with our dollar bill fare rolled up and sticking out of our noses (this practice had to be abandoned once Loonies were issued). It was powerful being that bizarre; people would immediately turn away, or get furious. To see an old man start cursing us just for singing and choreographing while waiting for a bus was an interesting view of lines of tolerance. Some folks get mad just because you're not like them.

One morning, in protest of the Club's new, earlier toilet cleaning schedule, we went to work in our pyjamas. It got a big laugh as we swept floors in floppy slippers, but of course one thing led to another, and we ended up partying in our pyjamas for two days at an MDA party. We passed out.

In the morning, there was a phone call from the Club. My parents had been trying to get a hold of me for hours, my boss

Lulu as Betty Bottomly.

informed me. My piano had arrived.

I struggled for a moment with this information. "Oh my God, is it Thanksgiving?" I moaned. I had told Mom and Dad that now that I was living in a house, I wanted my piano. They had driven it to Edmonton and had been waiting in the front yard of the house for two hours.

We called a cab, grabbed a couple of burly fags from the party and flew home like the wind.

Gloria and Lulu.

Mom's first view of Lulu was her slippered foot as she stepped out of the cab. Then I emerged. We had been in our pyjamas for two and a half days, and both wore sunglasses to hide our vibrating pupils.

We hauled my upright up the steps, my Dad and four fags. Inside the house, it became a distracting game of keeping Dad's attention from wandering to the elaborately framed drag photos of us on the mantel. I played for the first time in two years. Fingers slid magically into place, just like when I lived in Rocky. The room filled with the sounds of my favourite, dear, treasured friend.

I hadn't realized how much I had missed it.

Lulu and I were now regulars on the Flashback stage. The management didn't really get along with the reigning Mz., so we just started turning ourselves into stars. We would hang out on the loading dock, tormenting people and waving and hooting at the police when they cruised by. Lulu would hold the joint high and scream "Yoo-hoo! Husbands!" like she was daring them to arrest her. When I asked why she wasn't more careful she answered, "If they want to search you, tell them you're a sex

Gloria in various guises.

change and they have to send for a female cop. Most won't bother." We treated Flashback like our own private playground.

It was simple: no one ever said no.

Our first big show with our names on the poster was called "The Wild Sorority Sisters From The Planet Playtex Proudly Present: A Salute to Trailer Court Women." Our first real duet we did together was "Cry Me A River," closed-captioned for the thinking impaired (which meant I acted out every word in a made-up sign language). The act was designed to be a parody of Lindee Star and her twin brother, who would perform in real sign language. The effect was lovely (the first two or three thousand times), but Lulu and I usually had the most fun when it was at other people's expense. So we put our own version on stage, anticipating rage from the Old Guard for making fun of them.

That performance launched us into infamy.

The Empress Club didn't get it. But the audiences did.

The sight of Lulu lip-synching into a lime green toilet brush, or me teaching her how to give head on a zucchini won us quick acclaim.

But we weren't really crown material.

Yet.

So for a whole year we pushed limits, challenged Drag Authority, crossed every line of taste, and took over. The ruling Mz. Flashback was so scared of us that she ran from her own stage. We ran right on behind her and established a kind of renegade royalty: unelected but so firmly supported by the audience that no one dared challenge our authority.

We immediately set the plans in motion for our official arrival: May long weekend. The Coronation of the ninth Mz. Flashback.

I would be that Mz. Flashback.

Or, at least, that was the plan.

It wasn't as easy as we thought. A talented nobody named Twiggy almost beat me. But on voting night, I unleashed my secret weapon.

My number on voting night was a Sonny & Cher song. "I Got You, Babe." It was performed just like the end of their TV show: Mr. K. played Sonny and I was Cher, albeit a bargain basement version. Our costumes hadn't shown up and we were in a panic, throwing on whatever we could find in the knee-deep pile of tattered gowns that was the costume pit. We hit the stage desperate: Twiggy had received a huge round of applause for her performance. I had to top that or all of our carefully laid plans would be for nothing.

Gloria.

Lulu.

Gloria: The Value Village fashion show.

The music started. The crowd cheered as soon as they recognized the music, then screamed with laughter when the spotlight hit us. We looked like a bad Vegas version of a watered down caricature of a parody of Sonny & Cher. But that was fine: we knew our words and we launched into the routine with conviction, pretending we had meant to look that way, knowing all the while that we had the Mother of all big finishes in store.

We were nearing the end. The crowd was still with us. Then the loudest scream I've heard in my life erupted as our secret weapon hit the stage: Chastity.

Actually, a midget in drag dressed as Chastity.

The roar from the crowd obliterated the music completely. We stood on that stage, picked Chastity up in our arms, and smiled, like the perfect TV family. Chastity's monster sucker got stuck in my black wig and hung there, like a sticky, sugary earring.

We had crossed every line of taste in the book. And we won. That night I was crowned Mz. Flashback 9.

Standing on that stage, sculpted hair, lips quivering, arms stretched out at the stand-up mic, the spotlight cascading down then breaking like a million mirrors, refracted by my jewels until they were blinded, my eyes gazing upward, sparkling with life and emotion and passion for my separateness, my existence, that moment, like my entire life culminated on that stage, in that moment . . .

. . . that shining, perfect moment . . .

. . . the Applause.

With the crown on my head, we all piled into a big green van that had moved every drag queen in town at some point, and headed out to our first Tofield party.

You may want to pause and picture a convoy of wildly adorned she-males racing East to a rural setting to do the wildest drag show around. Legends abounded, tied together by traditions that went back to the house of Millicent herself. And the new Mz. Flashback was the Annual Guest of Honour.

The farm belonged to Rhoda B. and two lesbians. A modest place, but that part of the country saw some things that most farms can't even imagine. The house was a series of granaries and small trailers, attached in a crooked line with doors knocked out between them.

That night, as Lulu and I stood beside a bonfire so hot our bangs melted, guzzling Grand Marnier out of the bottle, our high heels sinking into the earth, she warned, "Whatever you do, don't pass out tonight. Evil events await the Mz. who cannot remain conscious throughout her Coronation." This wasn't going to be easy, as a good drag campaign is equal parts exhaustion, inspiration, and hallucination. It had been an entire week of shaving, cranking, painting and not sleeping. Already I was having trouble maintaining a vertical position without a birch to cling to.

Dozens of fags, dykes, and freaks wandered through the dark, back and forth between vans and campers, smoking drugs

Gloria and Twiggy: Halloween, 1986.

in the tree house, and apparently there was an orgy in the barn. But we had a show to do.

We made our way to the stage. When I saw it, my jaw dropped.

In a hollow in a field was a swampy dugout, four or five feet deep. The surface was thick with a dark green algae, the odd bulrush poking up out of the murky water. Around the pond, a dozen cars and trucks parked facing the water with their headlights blazing a makeshift spotlight. In the centre of the dugout was the stage: a floating raft of oil drums and plywood connected to the mainland by a long 2 x 4. On the raft stood Amii L. Nitrate, balancing precariously as she gesticulated, a full two seconds behind the tinny strains of "Somewhere Over the Rainbow" emanating full blast from a car stereo. The last thing I remember was Ginger Snot taking the big plunge in a wedding dress.

Bianca Bang-Bang said it best: "I know I'm in the country, but what country?"

I awoke with a start, hours later. Still in drag, in someone's living room, on someone's couch. A quick feel to the top of my head confirmed the worst.

My crown was gone.

I hastily searched the remnants of memories from the night before and came up empty. Then I heard laughter and realized there were people watching me. I looked around and saw Trash and Lulu, evil smirks on their faces.

"Lose something, Gloria?"

They led me back across the gravel road to the farm. A cow wearing a Dolly Parton wig ruminated glumly, watching us as we made our way to the chicken coop. There, glinting and sparkling in the early morning sunlight, high atop a power pole, sat the official Mz. Flashback crown. Thirty feet up.

I climbed up, like eight Mz. Flashbacks before me, and retrieved my prize.

I was one of them.

Sometime that same day, I read the beginning of the Creation of the Hole Family on a wall in the outhouse, penned by Ginger Snot sometime before she hit the brink in the dugout. Her stained wedding dress flapped on the clothesline.

The journey was under way.

If we could now get Lulu elected, we could control every drag event on every Big Onion stage for three solid years.

We could build a drag dynasty of entertainers that could rule the Big Onion for years to come. So we adopted queens left and right and created: The Hole Family.

And every once in a while—you created a monster.

And, of course, it happened one Halloween.

Excretia, 1983.

It Happened One Halloween

1984

LULU AND I SHOULD HAVE KNOWN you couldn't toy with the dark forces, especially on a night as potent as this. Were we playing Goddess? Perhaps. But like the most well-meaning of scientists, we were trying to use our powers for good and not for evil.

Girls just wanna have fun.

So we talked a mild mannered Maritime boy into crossing the line.

He didn't have to worry about a thing. We would personally supervise the transformation. With our combined talents and access to the Flashback costume pit, we would shape him into the most potent of punk priestesses. Lulu and I liked to believe we were the cutting edge of genderfuck drag. We would create her in our own image and send her forth to fly with the freaks.

Oh, the arrogance. Out-mothering mother nature is pure folly.

When we stepped back to survey our creation, a cold chill swept the room.

For there stood evil incarnate.

Fishnets shredded, then tied back together in a haphazard web. Tight black spandex mini. Bare midriff with a lean washboard stomach. Black lipstick. Black mask eye makeup and black cheekbones. White skin. A tire tube necklace with spikes protruding. Women's athletic hockey padding spray-painted black with studs and rivets and bolts instead of beads. Ripped fingerless evening gloves and black dragon lady nails.

Before us stood the Spawn of Satan in stilettos. Like Frankenstein's monster's fantasy bride, her hair swept straight up in a manic mohawk, reaching for heaven but rooted in Hell.

Then, like a low menacing growl from the very depths of depravity rising to the surface of our collective consciousness, her name sprung from our lips. Before we knew it, it had been spoken aloud, like a Spite released from Pandora's box. Irretrievable. Irrevocable. Unstoppable.

Excretia.

Excretia Nefarious Vulgaris. Keeper of the Royal Obscenities and Something Unspeakably Wicked. The Nuclear Waste Poster Child for the Nineties.

Under that calm male exterior seethed and bubbled a rage that, once unleashed, ran rampant through the night. Lulu and I gulped, and then did what all mad scientists must do.

We abandoned our creation and ran. Condemn us if you must. It was beyond our control.

That night she perched high on one of the stand-up bars, like a garish gargoyle, shrieking huge, swelling, opera diva screams over the pulsating technobeat, pausing to cross her eyes then flick a burning cigarette over the heads of the crowd. A beer bottle, when emptied, would be lobbed over her shoulder and into the mob. The world became her garbage can, a place to purge the piss and rage and fury and disgust with life. The universe. Everything.

Excretia didn't hate straight people. She thought everyone should own a couple. She lived to frighten them, and would do whatever it took.

Within a year, her name struck terror in the hearts of every hetero that walked into the place.

The world was fucked. And she was proof.

That night she reduced three straight chicks to tears, almost got punched out by one of their boyfriends, and stood in the bar lineup burning holes in some woman's fur coat while she chatted up her date.

Dragzilla on drugs. And we were Tokyo.

That night, she was born. Again.

That night she also picked up a cute straight boy while his

girlfriend wasn't looking and sucked him off in the downstairs can. They found him sitting unconscious on a toilet, jeans pulled down to his ankles, a ring of black lipstick around the base of his dick.

Strangely enough, some people were drawn to her seductively vile ways. The sheer sense of abandon in her tornado of terror sucked in the masochists one after another. She became the Demon Dominatrix, hypnotizing the unsuspecting like a Mad Max Medusa. In the arms of something wild and scary. Alien sex fiend on the hunt. Submit.

When Excretia disrupted our shows we stopped asking her to do them. But she didn't need the stage to perform. The Underground was her stage.

Excretia also fought with her own Drag Demon. With alarming regularity, she would swear off the whole scene, sometimes going as far as to burn all her drag, like she was exorcising the spirits that made her dress up.

But if it were that easy to quit, many of us would already have done just that.

The following Saturday would see her lurking near the dance floor, in a new outfit, chains rattling as she swayed, then thrashed to the music. We would all look the other way, hoping no one would point an accusing finger at us for not realizing the Fury we had set in motion.

Finally, she wearied of us and moved to Toronto to terrorize a whole new chunk of the world.

She scared us queens as much as anybody else.

Creation comes with a certain responsibility.

Empress I, Millicent, circa 1975.

In The Beginning

PEOPLE ALWAYS PREFER TALKING ABOUT YOU when you're gone.

Upon arrival in River City, my impressionable young mind was instantly deluged with a Noah-style flood of legends, myths, and glorious memories of faded grandeur.

It all began many moons ago when an Indian Princess planted her heel in the earth and declared herself Queen. Inspired by her might, hordes fell in behind her to cultivate the seeds of independence.

That Queen had a name.

Millicent.

She would be the only queen to simultaneously wear the Two Crowns of the Underground. And she would remind you of it every time she remembered it.

When Flashback was born, Millie was there, putting her name on the membership list before the paint on the dance floor had dried. By year's end, she had established two thrones and was firmly seated on both. For her efforts, she was immortalized.

Empress I, Mz. Flashback 1, the pushiest queen around: all still kowtowed to Millie. She was Unofficial Godmother to every queen I had ever met, partied with, or slept with. She was the Spirit of the Supremes half-bred with a shot of Indian Princess, shaken over ice, two straws. She breezed through every front door with the ease of a mountain wind, as familiar as sunlight. Drinks appeared like spirits on the bar in front of her, where her thin arms rested, manicured hand guiding a butch cigarette to her mouth, exhaling smoke signals to the patrons around her.

She held court wherever she sat, creating a powwow of

activity. Millie, being Number One, cherished all that she spawned. She called you by number, not by name, like a worried hen constantly taking attendance. She took an indirect kind of credit for every crowned queen in the Big Onion.

THE PARTY YEARS had taken their toll on Millie, who was nearly forty when I met her. I had guessed her age much higher; I hadn't learned yet that age was relative. She strolled through downtown as if she owned it, but of course no one that saw her knew that. They saw only a tired looking Indian man, like a hundred others you would see in a day. The only clue to her royal past was her nails: her pride and joy. They were long and immaculately manicured, at odds with her otherwise pedestrian appearance.

For Millie, the highest honour in the land was to be Empress. Or Mz. Flashback. The second you achieved either, your worth multiplied in her eyes. But as far as she was concerned, no one had ever been quite as fabulous as she remembered herself being. And because most of us were in grade school the first time she donned a frock, we were in no position to argue.

I would nod and smile whenever Millie boasted of her grandeur, not disbelieving, but skeptical. It was difficult to match the Myth with the frail man I saw in front of me. Then, at a party at her home, when she still had one, Millie pulled me to one side, secretively. She opened a photo album and showed me a black and white portrait of herself.

She was beautiful.

She wasn't in drag in the photograph. But she was a Queen.

Some men don't need to wear makeup to unleash their feminine side. I saw a proud, arrogant sideways glance at the camera, a tilt of the head, high sharp cheekbones, the hands placed just so. The two-spirited attitude dripped off the image.

I recognized the look: I had seen it many times in my own mirror as I tried to discover what I was.

I realized the only thing separating us was a few thousand bottles of rye.

Millie never really recovered from being Queen. Her year had been particularly rough: weeks after she and her Emperor had been crowned, he was arrested and charged with murder for some S&M sex that got out of hand. Millie, undaunted, finished her reign alone. Kingless. Regina Glorianna. Like Elizabeth I, Millie believed men were useful for guarding the crown, not possessing it.

She sat alone at her ball, throne centre stage. It was how everybody remembered her. Number One.

The candidates for the throne that year were Chatty Cathy Jackson and Grindl. Chatty was swept to power, and legend has it that Grindl, who had also lost the first Empress competition, died later that year under a table at a drunken party. Everyone thought that she had merely passed out, and continued to party around her. Hours later, when someone bothered to check, they finally called an ambulance and toasted her one last time.

Chatty went on to become the first Entertainer of the Year, and then the first Entertainer of the Decade. Millie went on to become the eternal dowager.

In her wake came all sixteen of us. The Empresses: Chatty Cathy Jackson, Nikki, Rayette, Trixie, Lindee Star, Mrs. K., Mary Mess, and Lulu LaRude. The Mz. Flashbacks: Felicia, Gino, Bianca Bang-Bang, Tina, Trash, Lexy Con and Gloria Hole.

By the time I became Number Nine, as she called me, Millie had stumbled down a few steps on the social ladder. Alcohol was rapidly becoming her main pastime. She no longer owned her own business; in fact, she had taken a position as co-toilet scrubber with Lulu and I at the Club. Us "new girls" at the bar were amused, to say the least, and Millie put up with more than her share of queen bitchiness. Dorky and I would draw little teepees and tomahawks on her time card. We constantly teased her about her age, and we never missed a chance to make fun of Diana Ross, Millie's idol.

Millie never fought back, just threatened revenge now and then.

We laughed, thinking that she would never bother.

Gloria.

A Legend

In Her Own Lunchtime

A GOOD QUEEN WAS JUDGED ALMOST ENTIRELY on the last week of her year of rule: Step-down Week. As the reigning Mz. Flashback prepared to bid her public farewell, the new candidates battled in the wings, ready to assume power.

Campaign Week.

This ritual was an intense one for several reasons. It was a double-edged kind of mood: relief and nostalgia; glory and sadness; the bittersweet feeling of something that feels so good, yet can't be over already, yet has to be.

Going out in style was the whole point.

Two Divas with Tiaras on their minds, battling publicly to rule the Underground: the ingredients of an exciting war. The public swarmed in behind their favourite, and the Battle Royale was under way.

The intensity of the experience was multiplied by the schedule: a manic, mesmerizing mayhem of nerves, passion, and drugs. The sheer number of shows in a campaign week was enough to make a hardened diva tremble.

The excitement all took place during the week leading up to the May long weekend, but preparations began back in March. First, to ensure the integrity of the Crown, some candidates had to be drummed up.

This choice had to be made carefully. Talent, youth and personality all had to be balanced with a real desire to represent the Club in the fashion to which it had become accustomed.

Flashback had the best queens, bar none. From the Grandeur of Millie, to the Wildness of Felicia, to the Seduction of Gino, to the High-Voltage Energy of Bianca Bang-Bang, to the Artistry of Gracie, to the Cult of Personality that was Tina, through the Insanity that was Trash, and finally the Timid Glamour of Lexy, the lure of the title of Mz. Flashback proved stronger than a young man's common sense or willpower year after year.

It wasn't just about the Crown, either.

The ranks of Flashback queens had a rich, varied history, and a nationwide reputation for performance on the edge. Many of the past rulers still performed, and when they hit the stage, confident that they no longer had anything to prove, the crowd cheered maniacally.

Those queens represented not just a fag bar, but a whole way of life: intense, popular, beautiful, mad, proud, and more fashionable than God ever intended.

When I stepped into the well-worn, hallowed pumps of my foresisters, Flashback was nearing the end of its first decade. A year later, the world was a different place. I was a different queen.

Power changes everything.

Lulu and I decided that nobody else was ready for that kind of power. As long as we controlled the Flashback stage, the Big

Gloria tries balloons.

Onion queens would be answerable to us. Lulu was becoming a phenomenon. She learned quickly what audiences were looking for and delivered it with feeling. She was the perfect blend of imagination and talent, with a touch of tragic heroine thrown in for dramatic effect. Her rise from the gutter touched people, and she had become the anchor of any show she performed in. I, on the other hand, was rapidly becoming the comic queen. Lulu and I hatched up some of the most demented performance drag anyone had seen. Our sphere of influence spread to Calgary, where we met the New Guard of the South. A wild family had also taken root there: The Del Rockos. Soon the Holes and the Del Rockos were inseparable. Flora Tron, Justine Tyme, Guy and Neon were changing the face of drag in the south. Cowtown, already cutting edge, went crazy when the Big Onion girls performed. Regular field trips between the cities strengthened our position as the premier entertainment dynasty in Alberta.

My first official appearance as the new Mz. Flashback was at the Calgary Ball. Lulu displayed me proudly, like a new pair of earrings. It was at that same ball that Lindee Star sold Entertainer of the Year to Lulu as they stole the Empress of Vancouver's rhinestone necklace from the trunk of a car. It was the first signal of an official thaw in the attitude toward Lulu from the Empresses.

That July, Lulu was appointed Entertainer of the Year. Halfway through her number (Bonnie Tyler's "Holding Out For a Hero"), her wig fell off. A gasp. She plunked it back on her head without missing a beat. The crowd roared. Lulu was poised to run again for Empress.

We sat in the drag pit one day, laying our plans.

"All we have to do," Lulu said, "is make sure the next Mz. Flashback is a member of the Family. She would still have to win the pageant on her own, but we could groom and assist her. Carefully," she added, remembering Excretia.

She took a huge drag off the joint we were smoking, then doubled over, coughing. This was normal. Then she refused the next toke. This was not. Complaining of a pain in her chest, she went back to cleaning toilets. (This was how we subsidized our drag habit: commercial sanitary engineers. Hardly glamorous, but essentially we got paid for cleaning up our own mess.)

Half an hour later, the pain still hadn't subsided.

When we got her to the hospital, we were told that one of her lungs had collapsed. She was admitted instantly.

The timing couldn't have been worse. Lulu's campaign for Empress IX was merely a month away, and she had a major public appearance coming up, playing Marilyn in a hair show. I

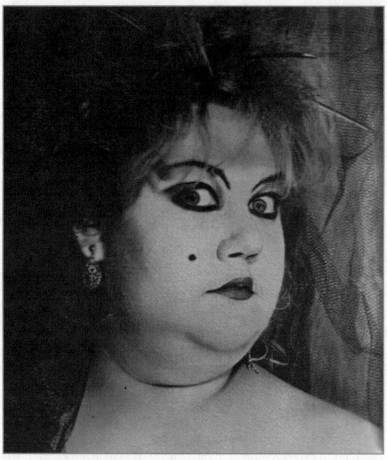

Neon.

Kim Burly in the Flashback kitchen.

immediately phoned Lindee Star to tell her the bad news: Lulu would have to be replaced.

Lindee suggested I take her place.

There are moments you remember all your life.

When I performed in Lulu's shoes that night (literally), I knew nothing would ever be the same again. Lindee did my makeup at the salon, I wore Mrs. K.'s white shimmy-fringe dress, I "borrowed" Tacky Tina's white feather boa from Lulu's drag pile, I performed for a sophisticated fashion crowd and they loved me. I was Jazz-Baby-Cocktail-Hour-Gin-Flavoured Fabulous as I worked the ramp to the strains of "Chicago."

I spent the night partying with some cute straight bartenders at Monroe's. A nineteen-year-old University hockey player told me I looked good enough to eat, and bought me Grand Marnier all night.

The next day, at the hospital, I filled Lulu in on what a fabulous evening I'd had. Maybe if I'd been paying attention, I'd have noticed the cloud of sadness behind her words of

Lulu.

encouragement. She asked me what I had worn. I told her. Then she chewed me out for borrowing a white feather boa without permission.

A crucial moment in a mother's life is when her first child stops needing her help to walk.

Lulu got out of the hospital just in time for the first campaign show. She stepped on stage in a full-length gown to hide the bandages. She never wore a backless gown again.

The crowd cheered, delirious with delight at her bravado, her circumstances, her timing. Her new appointment as Entertainer of the Year merely strengthened her position. Her competitor, Lori St. John, didn't stand a chance. You could just tell that it was Lulu's turn.

Mary Mess's ball theme was "Breakfast at Tiffany's." To most, that meant jewellery. To me, it meant wearing a large plastic fried egg on my head, woven into my Mz. Flashback crown. (Some people wear them on the inside, and some people wear them on the outside.) Mr. K. and I performed Sonny & Cher again, but the midget didn't show up, so it wasn't really as fun. By 11:00, Mr. K. had become Mrs. K. after a quick trip to his hotel room, and did his Empress Walk, and then hurried upstairs and got out of makeup and into black drag for her Command Performance. Mega costume changes are mandatory.

It wasn't much of a contest that year. Lulu won effortlessly.

She was crowned Empress IX at the Holiday Inn. The ballroom erupted with a roar of approval when the results of the voting were announced. She entered, the spotlight hit her, her beaded gown lit up the sky. She beamed radiantly, like a monarch gazing with love at her children, her people.

The crowd leapt to their feet. The crown was placed on her head. It looked like it had always belonged there.

Outside the Holiday Inn, the hookers, not all of them women, stood on the corner of boredom and desperation, unaware that inside, one of their own had transcended all that pain and reached the top. They bent down to look in the windows of the cruising station wagons. Sedans on the hunt. Some cars slowed down and some sped up and each got a wink or a finger and some came 'round again and some gave up. But no one stopped.

At the Victory Brunch the next day, Lulu broke with tradition, and instead of promoting Lori St. John, she appointed me her Imperial Princess. Second in line to the throne.

We had arrived. There would be no turning back.

And to the victor go the Girls. We were suddenly surrounded by queens eager to share the edges of that spotlight, as they simultaneously plotted to wear the crown next. Lulu started selecting her court from among the intriguers, as a stirring of Motherly instinct tugged at my cotton gusset.

My biological clock was ticking: drag time meant it was a bit behind schedule, but better late than never. I was halfway through my year, and it was time to start thinking about finding a successor, someone who would let us retain control. I took an interest in a fascinating work in progress. I was ready for my first child.

Tallulah.

ten nails,
two stilettos,
...and an attitude

TALLULAH

Tallulah.

Giving Birth Is A Messy Experience

1985

FOR TALLULAH, LIFE WAS FULL OF FIRSTS. An Italian Tundra Fairy from the word go, she had missed out on some fairly commonplace rites of passage for Canadian teenagers: driver's licences, school dances, horseback riding, bowling.

Growing up blind can't be easy. Growing up a blind epileptic overweight homo in Canada's North, next to impossible.

Yet, there she stood: jaw and cheekbones sharp enough to slice bagels, eyes painted à la silent movie star, a Cleopatra wig framing her face.

Dom Fatale. Leather mini. Black fishnets always always always. Film noir seductress as new wave '80s hooker. Uneasy, but strikingly easy.

She had designer friends. She wore designer clothes. She was designer drag.

Shiseido beard cover. Need I say more?

When Tallulah hit the stage, a life of cruel coincidence changed, finally, to a hope-filled Cinderella-type existence where dreams suddenly became possible. He who had never dared became She who never flinched: ten nails, two stilettos, and one Attitude. Her unique circumstances, and her general disdain of the tired drag we were trying to eliminate, made her a natural choice for inclusion into The Family.

I began tailoring her as the natural successor to my crown. The end of my reign was a few months away. Tallulah and I started performing together, creating demented events like the Value Village fashion show, but she was an uneasy comic. She eventually found her style: slut with an attitude. The crowd loved it. Then, something happened that every drag queen had been hoping for since the early seventies:

Tina Turner made a comeback.

Some careers are built on accidents of timing. Tina's comeback sent every queen in town racing for their long brown wigs and teasing combs. Tallulah beat them all to the stage, and claimed it for herself.

Thus a Diva was born.

We still had to talk her into running for the crown. It took about a month of promising that all she would have to do would be to show up and be fabulous before she finally relented and said yes.

I breathed a sigh of relief. I could now focus on Stepping Down, confident that the next phase of the Dynasty was in place. Assuming Tallulah won.

FLASHBACK. 1985, May long weekend. And I thought winning the crown was exhausting. Giving it away was worse. And, as luck would have it, my real family re-entered my life at the height of the madness.

A cousin was getting married. I was to play piano at her wedding. Of course, it was on the night of my Command Performance. My parents, in town for the wedding, knew better than to ask to stay with me, but they had been asking questions about my workplace. I deftly dodged their inquiries by vaguely alluding to a "show" I had to do later.

I arrived at Flashback wearing a suit. The wedding reception had run overtime, and I was way behind schedule. The rest of the girls were in drag, waiting impatiently. The Club was packed. I sat at the front of the stage with Mr. K. and we both lifted our glasses high, and the show began. We were the New Guard. And we flaunted it that night as The Family took to the stage: Lulu, our sister Flora Tron from Cowtown, Twiggy (my new aunt), Neon, Trash, and of course the candidates, our future, Dorky and Tallulah.

Dorky and Tallulah were running as a team for the Mr. and Mz. titles. Dorky was rapidly gaining visibility as the ultimate go-go boy. Night after night would find him in full view on the dance floor, dancing alone, a bright scarf jumping from hand to hand, lips turning blue from poppers. He often strolled through Flashback with Fluffy, a stuffed beagle that was more famous than any of us. Fluffy would follow Dorky through the mob, twelve feet behind his master, on a bright orange plastic leash. The crowd loved Fluffy. They would greet him as Dorky dragged him along the dance floor.

Fluffy ruled.

Tallulah seemed pretty much a shoo-in, but these things were never a sure thing. Her competition was Tinoir, a stunning tall black queen. Tallulah had more stage experience, but Tinoir had a knockout figure and looked much more convincing in drag. All week, the two performed, dragging out all their sure-fire finery, hungry for the win.

Tallulah and Gloria chat with an admirer as Ann and Nancy Wilson of Heart after the Women of Rock show.

It was still anyone's game.

We partied pretty hard that night. After the Club closed, Lulu and Flora, still in drag, were holding Amii L. Nitrate upside down on the bar with the booze pouring straight down her throat, while Neon, Dorky and I guzzled Schnapps and threw the shooter glasses against Gracie's mural. As we sat in the darkened Club after hours, one of Tinoir's campaign posters burst into flames. We all stopped in mid-chug and watched it burn.

We took it as an omen of Tallulah's impending conquest.

Then all I remember is holding on to a bench, trying not to fall off the planet. Sometime in the night, Lulu and Flora left, and I found my way to a toilet and dry heaved for a couple of hours. Holding on to that toilet, the cold porcelain against my forehead, still in my suit on the filthy floor, I made a drunken mental note to give Millie shit for not scrubbing underneath the toilets.

When Millie arrived to clean the Club, the front door was wide open. She ventured inside warily. Broken glass, lights on, music still playing. Other than that, nothing seemed out of

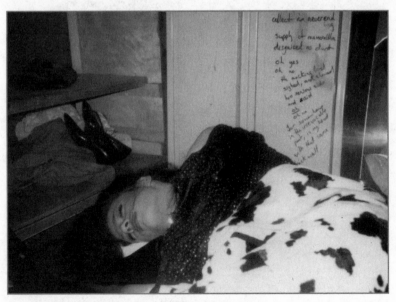

Gloria en repose.

order. She made coffee, sat down and lit an Export A with a trembling hand. She thought back to nine years ago when she herself had come to the end of her year in the spotlight. As her last act from the throne, she had refused to pass on the crown. The fledgling Club had been forced to scrape together the cash for a second crown.

She smiled. Then she wondered what happened to that crown . . . that all seemed like a lifetime away.

Finally she got up, filled a bucket and headed to the men's can. Then she screamed.

A pair of legs protruded from under one of the cubicles.

My legs.

Her scream woke me up. My suit was covered in chewing gum and god-knows-what-else. As I struggled to remember the night before, it gradually dawned on me that I had to crown the new Mz. that night. I was looking at a fourteen hour day, half of it in drag, and I was waking up in broad daylight around a toilet in a fag bar men's room with no idea what time it was.

I STUMBLED to action. *Those bitches deserted me!* I realized. Then, as I called a cab, Millie's scream rang out once more.

On her way through the drag room in the dark, Millie had tripped over a body.

It was Neon. Still dressed as Divine, half her face smudged on the drag room carpet, cuddled up to our stage dummy. Both blanketed in pink fun fur.

As Neon and I returned home in the taxi, I was fuming. The cabbie stared covertly into the mirror, probably watching for early signs of nausea. The sunlight burned through the windshield, Neon slumped against the window of the cab, her makeup leaving a huge streak on the glass. We drove past churchgoers on the way to worship; they stared at us as the cab drove by. Once at the apartment, I got even more hysterical. There was no place to sleep; drag queens lay everywhere, and Lulu and Flora had stolen my bed. Neon fell asleep on the floor. I took a shower, grabbed my drag bag, tiara, and stepping-down gown, and headed back to the Club to prepare for the Drag Races.

The Drag Races did not involve high-speed cars. They were more like a Cross-dresser's Olympics.

Every May long weekend, Flashback prepared for the onslaught of madness. Before the Step-down, before the Crowning, before the queens painted, the staff would arrive, clean the Club, warm up the barbecue, and fill up the dunk tank. The alley was blocked off at both ends. The beer cooler was stuffed with wading pools full of lime JELL-O, and I was going over the list of events for the day:

Tug-of-War, Wet T-Shirt, Wet Jockstrap, Skiing for Five, Run Like a Girl / Boy, Waitress races, Pie Eating Contests, Condom Blow-up, JELL-O Wrestling (later it became Creamed Corn Wrestling), The Foxy Lady Rhinestone Turkey Baster Relay Marathon, The Squeeze-a-Snack Relay Marathon, The DQ Dunk Tank, The Lady Di Faint-a-Like Contest, and of course, The Drag Races, which involved running back and forth in the deep gravel in the alley, gradually layering on women's clothing from the Drag Pit. Naturally, maximum liquor intake was mandatory.

I poured a huge Tanqueray and supervised production. Once satisfied that everything was under control, I went into the men's can and performed the Big Shave. On a day this tightly scheduled, one had to plan ahead.

Then I counted the votes. Voting had occurred two nights earlier. The ballots were sealed in the office credenza, and nobody knew for the weekend who would win. I watched as Tallulah pulled ahead, then fell behind Tinoir. Unfolding and tallying the crumpled drunken ballots, I gradually saw The Family pull into a comfortable, then an unbeatable lead.

We had done it. My daughter would receive the Crown.

I pictured the moment when I would pin the Crown into her wig. My bosom swelled with motherly pride as I imagined it.

People were now arriving at the Club. The alley was gradually filling up with buffed boys in obscenely short cut-offs, loud queens from Edmonton and Calgary, dykes in muscle shirts, and the crowd of fans that populated every drag event. Dance music blasted into the alley, and people streamed in and out of the Club, carrying booze in plastic cups. Now and then a civilian would walk by, peer into the alley, and walk away with a confused look on his face. Or a Chinese family of eight would stop and watch for an hour, commenting to each other and laughing. Rhoda B., the essential Drag Races Emcee, was screaming into a microphone, cajoling people into entering events with strings of insults, bribes, and threats.

Lulu and Flora arrived with Neon. Their hangovers could only be described as epic. They ordered drinks and we got all the rhinestone jewellery for the show together and ran it through the dishwasher. Millie stood with the other Dowagers (has-beens), avoiding direct sunlight. She was already drunk, even at this early hour, and was laughing and telling everybody how she had found me this morning. Tallulah and Dorky showed up, their nerves frazzled. I wanted so badly to tell them they had won, so they could relax and have fun with no pressure. Then I remembered how it felt when they called my name, a year ago, and decided that a little mental torment would build character. They mingled.

Just as the Wet Jockstrap contest started, there was a phone call for me in the office.

My parents. "We were looking for the bar you work at, but all we could find at that address was an alley full of . . . well, I'm not sure . . ." Mom's voice trailed off.

I froze. They were at the phone booth down the street. No escape.

Mom and Dad's first view of the people I worked with was a bunch of pretty boys in jockstraps being hosed down, goose bumps raising, testicles shrinking, while drunken fags screamed with delight. I quickly led them inside and got them a beer. They stood and watched the mayhem, expressions of disbelief on their faces.

I realized the only thing connecting our two worlds at the moment was the river that ran between their home and mine.

Rhoda B. emcees the Drag Races.

How could I explain that I didn't really want them to see this? How to explain the importance of this day for me, the metamorphosis of me into a respected dowager, the year of change and growth that I had just passed through?

How to explain that this was a Family moment? My triumph, my journey, was nearly complete, and I couldn't find the words to explain to them what they were seeing? Until this period of change was over, I couldn't afford to have them invade my new world.

How do you tell your family that they don't belong in this picture?

Mom and Dad were polite. They made conversation with a few of the gang, but they left after they were done their beer, without saying much. I watched them leave with relief. My attention, until now divided, returned to the task at hand.

Now I was behind schedule. Lulu and Tallulah were already painting in the Drag Pit. I joined them. Outside, the mayhem continued, as the queens prepared to dazzle indoors.

The actual show is a bit of a blur: too many hallucinogens, no doubt. All I really remember is my final performance as Mz. Flashback.

Every queen develops a repertoire over time. You try many things, and sometimes they don't pan out. When you find an act that makes the audience giddy with delight, you milk it for all it's worth. And one of my performances had quickly become legend Underground. The song: Shirley Bassey's *"This Is My Life."*

A drag standard from the live recording, the song was about affirmation of values, strength of conviction, singleness of purpose, defying naysayers, and forging your own road.

In my hands, it became a commercial for Life Brand cereal.

Picture a glam Vegas-style apparition in a floor-length gown, belting as only Bassey can, recorded applause thundering approval with every emotional crest of the music. Now add a giant bowl of breakfast cereal in milk, and watch the fun begin.

In my short career so far, it had become a trademark performance, and my one and only consent to the Glamification of Gloria.

The audience, as always, recognized the music immediately. (They usually knew the lyrics as well as we did.) I sat on a chair, delivering meaningful, pensive glances with mock seriousness. Then, at a pre-arranged cue, Lulu entered with a giant punch bowl and set it in my lap. I continued emoting. Lulu re-entered with a box of Life cereal just as I hit the chorus. She poured it into the bowl, then added a gallon of milk. There I sat, in my custom-made gown, banner across my foamies, crown in my hair, with a sloshy bowl of what was rapidly becoming porridge in my lap. The music crested to its big finish, the orchestra punched the final chords, and the audiences, both canned and live, erupted with approval.

I sat soaking up the applause. This was the moment I had been waiting for all year: the spotlight cascading down, a stunning outfit, an amazing crowd drunk with delight as they bid me farewell. And of course, a video camera filming the entire spectacle, preserving this glorious moment forever.

Millie approached the stage. The first Mz. Flashback and the current Mz. Flashback onstage together: the Past meets the Present to greet the Future. She stood next to me and leaned over to kiss me on the cheek.

The next few seconds replay in my mind like a scene from a

Gretchen and the infamous tampon swing dress.

bad horror movie. Millie reached down, lifted the punch bowl full of cereal and milk, and dumped it over my head.

A roar of laughter, then shocked silence, a gasp that still resounds in my ears, trapped on video for all time.

I sat frozen. My hair, coiffed exquisitely, now hung in drippy tendrils. Droplets of milk sparkled in the spotlight. Little bits of porridgey wheat croutons clung to my crown, the very crown I was about to place on my daughter's head. My mascara ran down my cheeks in black teary lines, proving that "waterproof" on the label of something is as misleading as "one size fits all."

In my imagination, the doors all slam shut, the lights go out, and my telepathic rage wreaks havoc on everybody who has ever tormented or laughed at me.

By the time I came back to reality, Millie was gone, chased out of the Club. And I was centre stage with a fag bar full of people so quiet you could have heard an earring drop.

The proceedings came to a standstill while the stage was mopped. Someone threw a paisley bathrobe over my soggy shoulders. The crown was run through the dishwasher. Tallulah's name was announced, and she hit the stage, glamorous, smile beaming bright enough to light up the Tundra. She took one look at me and burst out laughing.

After I pinned the Crown into her wig, she wouldn't even hug me. I was getting sticky.

Out in Tofield that night, I managed to get the Crown back. I climbed the pole in the chicken coop, and, knowing how afraid of heights she was, placed it on the very top.

Zola and Cleo step down (only later did they realize that the pig's ears were real).

Standing on the ground, I watched it as the sun rose. Once the sky was at its brightest, a shaft of sunlight collided with the big centre rhinestone.

It shone like a star that had something to announce: an arrival.

A Birth.

I turned and joined Lulu and Ginger Snot in the outhouse. They were already writing the next chapter on the wall, giggling hysterically. Lulu turned to me. "Gloria, how do you spell placenta?"

Iris Shopashinsky in the drag room.

Armageddon

July 1, 1985

FLASHBACK. THE DRAG ROOM. A long mirrored tunnel under the sound booth filled with skinny pasty boys. None of us *ever* saw the light of day. We were the boys who put the vamp in vampire. Sunlight touched us only when we rolled out of the bar at 10:00 AM. The only colour in our cheeks was the stuff we painted on.

Lulu was stepping down as Entertainer of the Year. When she received the award we took it as a validation of our style of drag. We were now recognized as the New Wave. The old guard gave up trying to stop the revolution and embraced our innovations with a smirk of distaste, not realizing that the award would now remain in The Family for years to come. Who received the glory next was entirely up to Lulu.

And she wasn't talking.

Who would she choose? We were all in the running. Tallulah? Twiggy? Me? I was the main contender. And her best friend. And her roommate, but the roommate politics could work against me.

The show is already an hour late. Out in the bar, nobody notices.

Nerves frazzle on contact. It's a big night. All are applying makeup. Fanning lashes to dry the glue. Slipping on pair after pair after pair of nylons. In the hairspray-face-powder-perfume-cigarette-smoke-body-odour-choked air, curses and giggles and boyisms and girlisms bounce off the makeup mirror. Queens are mean, but before they take it out on you, they warm up on each other.

Tallulah was a changed queen. Unafraid, the boy who had to be talked onto the stage had become gutsy, daring, and original.

Iris, Kim Burly, John Reid and Gloria party in the kitchen.

She had a crown now. The pressure to impress meant you worked harder, danced faster, went the extra mile. This pageant was her first important showcase since winning.

She was doing Grace Jones for the first time.

Watching a five foot ten Italian boy transform into an avant-garde Amazon Negresse takes some imagination in the early phases.

First: Erase the face. Glue painted over the brows. Avocado beard cover. (Tallulah was Italian. Three words: one o'clock shadow.) Then a deep brown base. Now, of course, when you do cross-racial cross-dressing (in the old days it was just called black chick drag) every piece of exposed skin has to be darkened. For Tallulah's debut as the disco diva: a sequin tube top. And leather micro-mini. And little leather glovettes. This meant shoulders, back, armpits, face, neck, ears and midriff all had to be painted. And Tallulah was behind schedule. And crabby.

Iris floats in. Late. Lulu bitches at her because it's her show and she can, and Iris always kind of inspires that kind of abuse. We call her Virus.

Iris was an artist who never quite got the hang of doing drag. Not to be confused with a drag queen who never quite got the

Gretchen and Twiggy (de-frocked) in the drag room.

hang of being an artist. They're at least pretty. Sometimes.

There's no room for Iris at the head mirror and we don't really want her there so we send her back to get ready by the janitor sink we all pee in before the show. Definitely B-list.

Twiggy arrives. Also late, but we like her. She had turned out to be not just a worthy opponent, but definite Hole Family material. She was adopted as a sister of Lulu. Twiggy needed no mother, as there wasn't a lot you could teach someone like that. Slender, sophisticated, sparkly. Our star dancer. She does things in heels that no woman would dare. Ex-Arthur Murray dance instructor reborn as Judy Garland's only talented daughter. *Not* Liza. We make room at the head mirror. Definitely A-list.

Tallulah's finally covered in black base so she gets ready to draw eyebrows.

Then she realizes that her hands are already covered in the stuff, meaning everything she touches will be covered in brown smudges. Clothes, makeup, everything. She lights a cigarette to calm down.

The show is now two hours late. Out in the bar, nobody notices.

Twiggy's gossiping about Iris. Turns out when Iris's roommate

Neon in the drag room.

Lori St. John was in the hospital, Iris pawned off all the furniture, appliances, even the fish tank. None of which belonged to her. She was probably wearing the profits right now in the form of that new beaded disaster of a gown she arrived in, illustrating once more that taste and price don't always travel together.

This amuses all of us greatly, except Tallulah who's just in a pissy mood. She heads to the janitor sink to wash her hands. Then Twiggy prances out for a shooter at the bar. Then Tallulah storms back in a rage because Iris won't move to let her clean up. Then the door flies open and Twiggy appears with a wild panicked look and is about to say something, some kind of warning, when she trips on her marabou cape and plunges in a sparkling heap to the foot of the stairs. We all jump up and run to her. We form a circle to pick her up and get her to a chair. Her ankle is fucked.

Just as we heave—the door opens again and two police officers step into the drag pit.

The room falls completely silent except for the subtle crinkle of plastic as someone discreetly tucks a bag of pot into a bra. Eight queens in various states of readiness, most in nothing more than pantyhose and dance belts, almost all with some kind of outstanding warrant, look up at them.

The cops scan the room. The walls are covered in graffiti, Diana Ross posters, headdresses and autographs. The eyes looking back at them are heavy, dark, harshly powdered. You can never wear too much Brigitte Bardot Black.

Someone makes a "yummy yummy" kind of predatory noise at the back of her throat. It's for cop number two, a strapping tall young blond demigod in uniform. Lulu lights up a cigarette, squeezes a breast into shape and strikes a pose. "Well, if it isn't the husbands. Whatcha lookin' for, boys?" She exhales into the already smoky air and steps up to them, all seven feet and two hundred plus pounds of her. She towers over both of them, completely filling the space between floor and ceiling. She gazes down at the older cop's bald spot.

In his best official unflustered voice, cop number one, an older, married seen-it-all kind of guy says "We're looking for a Mister—." And then he says a man's name.

Understand, for a moment, that in the drag world, boy names just never came up. We had spent years as Twiggy, Gloria, Lulu, Tallulah. It's all we knew. So it took a moment. To register.

Then a collective rush of realization: They were looking for Iris.

Everyone goes on naive mode. We've got the home advantage. We know that even if Iris walks into the room, she's in drag. They won't recognize her. Unless someone tells.

It's an interestingly powerful position to be in. We could pull the wool over the eyes of Edmonton's finest. That would be cool. Or we could send Iris off to spend the night in jail. In drag.

Also cool.

And just as we all sit pondering what not to say, Tallulah, for whom tact was rarely considered, screamed "Virus, there's some visitors here for you."

There's something titillating about watching a lanky blond cop handcuff a drag queen. Even when it's Iris. There, but for the Grace of God . . .

Iris didn't do the show that night. She spent the next twelve hours in a holding cell in full gear. Not an experience for the faint of heart. The lighting is merciless and by the time you're processed, your beard is growing through.

Or, at least, that's what I've heard.

Twiggy did do the show that night. Fucked ankle and all. She changed into something floor-length, we carried her to centre stage and she did a Streisand stand-and-quiver kind of

Cleo (de-frocked) and Justine Tyme in the drag room.

performance. The audience cheered, she bowed, and we carried her off.

Tallulah didn't do the show that night. By this time she was so far behind schedule and so stressed out that none of us should have been surprised when her epileptic seizure started. At the mirror, she dropped her black liner, her hand started to vibrate, then her arm spasmed and she fell back in her chair, pulling the makeup counter over on her way down. She's on the floor in a pile of tackle boxes and colour palettes, doin' the old grand mal.

The six remaining queens start screaming and running around. Red Cross didn't teach blending, so none of us went.

Finally, a doctor in full leather gear came in to help. An hour later, she was driven home wrapped in a bathrobe. Still black. She slept for two days and then woke up. Not black. Her bedding, however, was a different story. She didn't remember a thing.

The first thing she asked me was whether or not she had won.

I had to tell her Lulu had given me Entertainer of the Year that night.

Tallulah was furious. She had wanted that one badly. But after a four hour fight, we ordered pizza and made up. I also promised her I would give her the title when I stepped down. I had that kind of Power now.

Life with Lulu had become exclusive. We literally spent every second of every day together, planning shows, plotting schemes, deciding who would be the next Superstar, grooming successors. But often, we would argue about the other's choices. She was still perceived as the leader in most circles, despite the fact that I was officially the boss on the stage we all lived to perform on.

Lulu didn't know it yet, but by naming me her successor she had just committed the biggest mistake of her drag career. I had two crowns now. We were even once more.

The music from that performance still rings in my ears.

As I performed that night, hoping against hope that I would win, flipping my hair around, trying out my more serious, sexy side, I was already dreaming of the day when I didn't have to share that spotlight with anyone.

Despite all the chaos backstage, we all performed our asses off that night. The show ended up going on three and a half hours late, but it was a drag show.

Nobody noticed.

Gloria and Lulu, a classic mother-daugher pose.

Two Men Enter—One Man Leave

September, 1985

LULU STEPPED DOWN AS EMPRESS A FEW months later. It was the Ball of the decade (literally: the Tenth Year of Glamour had begun). The theme was 'Let Them Eat Cake,' and our first entrance was as The Royal Wedding Party, with Lulu as the blushing bride, and Tallulah, Twiggy, and I as her bevy of virgins-in-waiting. To make things unusual, I wore a Walkman and listened to my own music as we performed "Goin' to the Chapel   Boogie Woogie Bugle Boy." As Imperial Princess, I stood next to my Dragmother on the Dais all night, receiving out-of-town dignitaries, watching as platitudes and gifts were showered at Lulu's feet, mopping her brow to preserve her makeup till her Final Walk.

The candidates for Empress were Amii L. Nitrate and Lori St. John, fresh out of the hospital minus part of a leg, back for another challenge. Lori's diabetes had landed her in surgery to amputate a foot. She simply switched to flats and moved on.

Ball weekend. It was what we lived for.

Picture two or three floors of a downtown hotel, the Holiday Inn again in this case, packed with room after room of men with far too much luggage, tweezed eyebrows, garment bags and loud voices, bustling from suite to suite to "borrow" drag essentials, share beauty tips and drug connections, and basically crank till you drop. The Empress is the star of the entire week.

The big ballroom is decorated, multiple spotlights in place, video cameras poised to catch the proceedings. At one end of the ballroom stands the dais, on a dramatically lit stage, with two thrones and some extra seating for the prince and princess, along with some celebrity out-of-town dignitaries. A long runway extends from the dais down the middle of the ballroom, with tables surrounding it Las Vegas style.

The Ball is part Ritual, part Fashion Show. The Empress is part politician, part photo opportunity.

Being the most fabulous was the entire name of the game.

There was a fair amount at stake, too. Canada was currently run by the youngest Empresses on record. Lulu, Calgary's Flora Tron and Vancouver's Christopher Peterson were a mere twenty years old when they ascended the throne. This Western Canadian Triad was knocking the American Empresses out of the way, receiving standing ovations at all the Balls south of the border. We had something to prove. We were young and adventurous. And thin.

A LARGE number of Americans were at Lulu's Ball. She had made quite an impression in cities like Spokane and Seattle, and the Empress Club responded by travelling north, where the Big Onion Queens were rapidly developing a reputation as

Tallulah.

the wildest party children of all Canada.

The Ball started late, naturally, but by the middle of the first set of Entrances, the ballroom was packed. The lobby of the hotel was filled with curious onlookers as the Queens strutted their stuff. The elevator doors opened, and impossibly large creatures emerged, grandly sweeping across the floor toward the ballroom. The air filled with the shrieks of adoration as mutual compliment trading occurred, everyone's voice acquiring a more epic tone of hysteria, as befits an occasion of such majesty. Every ding of the elevator signalled another flood of taffeta-rhinestone-hairspray creations, until the entire main floor was submerged in headdresses and leather and capes and crowns.

Even Millie was coming out of a four year hiatus and donning a frock for the event.

The big buzz of the evening, however, was Tallulah.

The Flashback Entrance at any Ball was one of the highlights of the evening. Everyone knew what Tallulah was planning: Thunderdome had recently hit the theatres, and we had all seen the video. A post-apocalyptic Tina Turner stood against a fiery smoky sky, encased in futuristic chain mail mesh, belting "We Don't Need Another Hero." Tallulah had the dress copied, and the ballroom sat in breathless anticipation. Then, the unthinkable happened: minutes before Tallulah was scheduled to hit the ramp, we heard her music start.

Tallulah performing Thunderdome, 1984.

Empress I Millie and Empress Regent X Mother Jean.

Lulu and I looked at each other in horror. Repeat drag numbers at a ball were fairly common until we came along; but this was a Family moment, and some Empress from Spokane was stealing our thunder. Lulu froze with a smile on her face (she had to be polite), and I just stared at the stage.

Out in the lobby, the elevator opened and Tallulah stepped out. She heard her music coming from the ballroom, and had a moment of panic as she assumed it was hers. She ran to the entrance and saw her number being done by somebody else.

The old Tallulah would have taken one look at the ballroom, turned on her heel, and fled back to her hotel room.

But this was a queen with a crown now. One look in the full-length mirror in the lobby confirmed it.

The music in the ballroom ended to polite garden applause. A tepid response at best. Then, immediately after, the song started again. Tallulah stepped into the ballroom.

The audience leapt to its feet.

Tallulah was a reincarnation of Tina's Thunderdome character. Silver metal mesh draped off her shoulders, reinforced with armoured bra, silver gloves, and a platinum mohawk crowning her head, then cascading down her back.

She stood in the double spotlights and fireflies of light flew off her frame and shimmered on the walls of the ballroom. With every chorus, her silver fist shot into the air in a gesture of defiance.

Goosebumps.

On the dais, Lulu and I looked at each other and smiled.

Amii L. Nitrate became Empress X. We would all soon be sorry. Poor Lori St. John retreated again into obscurity. She would have to find another way to make her mark on the world.

Amii lasted a few months as Empress, then cracked from the pressure, abdicated, and moved to Saskatchewan, where she opened a hair salon and ran for Empress again eventually. It was a rocky shift of decade, and no one could have anticipated what happened next.

The crown was passed to Mother Jean, an eighty-year-old woman who had been a fixture in the Underground since the days of Millicent. She was, and is still, the only woman to wear the Big Onion Crown.

There is much that could be said about the age-old relationship between a straight woman and a gay man. Intensify all of that, and you might understand the connection between some straight women and drag queens.

Mother Jean was a dear friend of Millie's in year one. Because of her constant emotional support through the years and her tireless vigilance fighting for respect for the drag community, she was given the title Imperial Gay Mother Of All Alberta. She brought a lot of dignity to the throne that year. She was the proudest Empress Regent that there could have possibly been.

She could also pack away more rye than any of us on a given night.

Rayette (Lola St. Clair) with a very young Lulu.

Little House On The Prairie

1984–1986
11415–100 Avenue

TO TRULY UNDERSTAND A SPECIES, find out where it lives.

A drag house is an easy one to spot. It will be a large, prominent structure. Corner lot, probably with a dramatic entrance or turret or balcony or something fabulous about it. Chances are, if it looks like a scene from a costume epic could be filmed in the yard, it's rented by queens.

Never just one. Always a group. Usually about the same age, philosophy, and build. If all the queens were the same size, you could quadruple your drag wardrobe.

When Trash approached us one day and said that she had found the most amazing house and would we move in with her, we shrieked with delight.

Lulu and I teamed up with Trash to become the founding Mothers of Walla Walla West. Within a year, the address could make a cabby quake with fear.

Lulu and I packed our things, said goodbye to Annie Hole and Joolz, and headed to the new house. The first load of junque filled the big green van. The piano was loaded into the back of a truck, with me fretting over it, sitting by its side. Lulu held on to the other side. She talked me into playing something while we drove. I launched into "Cry Me A River," and Lulu sang into the rhinestone turkey baster with a white feather boa flapping in the wind.

No stage was too small, especially if it was on wheels.

Who moved in next depended on what we needed most. The population of Walla Walla West swelled at times from five to eleven queens, depending on who Lulu was feuding with, or how close Ball Weekend was. As the ruling queens, we hosted

Ora en repose.

most of the out-of-town Empresses when they visited.

We invited a post-apocalyptic punk poet queen named Iona Box, and Prickles, an ex-queen with a drinking problem, to join us. They seemed to balance things quite nicely. Iona immediately insisted that we take down all the porcelain Pierrot clowns that Lulu collected. Iona had a phobia about clowns: they gave her nightmares. She had never been to a McDonald's for that very reason.

When Iona unpacked, we saw a baby's headstone among her things.

We didn't ask.

The future seemed a million spotlight years away, but Lulu had hers all figured out. "When I'm sixty-five I'm getting a sex change, 'cause everyone hates a dirty old man, but everyone loves a dirty old woman."

During the week, things were fairly normal. We worked our various waitress jobs, hung out at the bar, even had a bit of a day schedule. Lulu and I would take the bus to work on cold mornings, and watch all the normal people scurrying to their normal jobs in their normal clothes, and wonder where we fit into the grand scheme of things. Looking around, it was easy to believe we were all aliens, like Iona said. There weren't a lot of people like us, it seemed.

Then on the bus one morning, Lulu nudged me. "There!" she said excitedly, "There we are! That's us!" I looked.

Two ancient old ladies stood on the corner. One was nearly

blind, the other curved over until she was half her size. They held onto each other as they crossed the street, achingly slow, each trusting the other to guide or support. The world rushed past them while they lived frozen in time, like two ancient sisters dressed for presentation. Or preservation.

Iona Box.

Alone in the world.

But we were never alone on the weekend. The neighbours could usually hear the hum of activity on a Saturday morning. Bette Midler's "Live at Last" double album would waft on clouds of marijuana smoke into the alley at the crack of noon. It was required learning for every queen—memorize every joke and song. As the day wore on, boys would start arriving on foot or by cab, carrying wigheads, bags of pantyhose, or dresses that blinded you in the sunlight.

The living room became the Follies' rehearsal hall. Move the couch and coffee table to one side and work it, girls. In one afternoon we could choreograph the opening and closing production numbers. By the end of it, all are exhausted and sweaty, sitting around in stubble and pumps, listening to the same song over and over and over, lip-synching quietly to ourselves and smoking.

Then—the painting began.

For the neighbours, this ominous silence was a warning. Only one thing could require that kind of silent focus. One by one the wigs in the upstairs window would disappear.

It must have looked strange to the neighbours. Every

Saturday, eight men would arrive. You would never see them leave.

Two or three cabs would pull up to the house, the front door would open and a parade of huge, feathered, shiny freaks would emerge, snake through the front yard and cram itself into the taxis, trying not to crush, fold, bend, or wrinkle anything. Not an easy task. The bigger the hair, the closer to God.

Then . . . hours of silence. The evening ticked by. The neighbours would go to bed.

At 5:00 AM, an ungodly screech would slice through the night. It was usually Lulu announcing to the world that we were home, but it could have easily been Ora or Trash or Tina or Iona or Prickles or Neon or Reena or some out-of-town Empress or all at once. The house would explode with life and noise and punk rock and disco and occasionally a brawl or a person falling through a plate glass window. Flashback would empty its entire contents into our house. Skinheads and models and junkies and

Dorky being Dorky.

leather queens would head for Walla Walla West. Four floors of party ambience: the main floor had the draft keg in the kitchen, the loudest music, a piano, lots of mannequins and unmatched lamps, and dozens of defunct telephones.

Dorky being Louise.

The second floor was bedrooms, each uniquely spectacular in its own disarray. The attic was like a huge drag fort. Trash held court here, supervising the wandering guests. The basement was usually where the hard core druggies hung out.

Amityville.

And everywhere you looked on every floor—drag. We lived knee deep in it.

As real people would wake and look out of their windows, they would see a four-car taxi lineup in front of the house, a yard littered with unconscious bodies draped fetchingly, Prickles stumbling and mumbling into people spilling flat beer wherever he went, Lulu on the back balcony in leopard sunglasses and a pink princess gown screaming hello to the sun. Iona would be reading snark poetry in the kitchen, and I would be upstairs working on my favourite blond boy.

Those were the days.

We were gradually turning drug use and partying into an art form. The menu from those days reads like a who's who of stimulants: liquor, bennies, pot, acid, MDA, poppers, the occasional cocaine, speed, mescaline, nicotine, caffeine, sugar, sex, and of course, mushrooms. Our marijuana dealer lived two doors down, and many a morning would find one of us clad only in a bathrobe, tiptoeing down the street with a coffee cup in hand, needing to "borrow a cup of reefer."

Ora and Gloria at the back bar.

One weekend at the bar, one of the managers gave us some mushrooms that had been confiscated from one of the patrons. If there was anything we appreciated, it was free narcotics. We decided to brew a pot of tea, thereby ensuring that everyone hanging with us that night would get some. We were poor, but generous. We partied all night, laughing and hallucinating. The mushrooms were some of the strongest I'd ever had; hours went by, morning came and we were still flying. Then Iona decided to go and buy cigarettes. She put on a stupid hat for effect, then stepped outside.

Seconds later, she was back, in a total panic. "The house is surrounded by cops!" she screamed, locking the door behind her.

We laughed, thinking she was just trying to be funny. Then Trash looked out the living room window. "Oh my God, she's right," she muttered.

We stopped laughing, then raced up to the attic, which had a full view of the street. Indeed, there were cops everywhere. But as we watched, we realized they weren't casing out the house. The police stood on guard every half block, standing, staring straight ahead. As far as we could see, the neighbourhood was fortified. But why?

We went downstairs and brewed more mushroom tea. Now that peril was no longer imminent, we could return to our plans. Then someone flipped on the television, and we saw the Pope landing in the Big Onion.

And the Basilica he was heading for was a mere three blocks from Walla Walla West.

Gloria rocks the Toronto Ball.

We began selecting outfits for a Papal audience.

Nothing like a tiny act of defiance to get you through the day. Of course, we knew we wouldn't get to meet him. But how many chances do you get at freaking out *that* audience? And of course, we didn't do drag. We just wanted to dress like aliens and see how people would react. We finished our tea and headed out.

The Big Onion had done its best to prepare for the Pope. All along the Popemobile's route, graffiti had been painted over, walls decorated, reality prettied up, the surface of the city polished, denying the existence of anything ugly or obscene or deviant. All along Jasper Avenue, parade seating was set up, packed with anxious Catholics for hours before he arrived. Police stood on rooftops, armed. Heavily, it seemed. The air was thick with a deep, powerful authority, the sky rumbled and churned with clouds, and suddenly, being an obvious freak seemed dangerously close to public suicide. We surveyed the scene from the Mac's parking lot where Lulu and I had fought off the fag bashers, and we all removed our ladies' hats, cat-eye glasses and jewellery, and put them in our coat pockets.

This was definitely not the time.

"Keeping the faith certainly takes a lot of artillery," observed Iona.

"We can't see a thing from here. Let's go further down the street, and maybe we'll catch a look at the Popemobile," said Lulu. We moved past the street vendors hawking icons and souvenir Pope Plates, and eventually found a spot a few blocks down.

A hush fell over the crowd. Then the sky darkened, and we heard a helicopter approaching. It swooped down the street, roaring, clearing the way, followed by a rank of black motorcycles, some black cars, then finally . . .

The Popemobile sped into view, a plastic bubble in the back of a van with a little white man waving robotically, gone before the crowd could do anything but gasp and race after him.

We stood still as people ran past us excitedly. We may not have felt the faith, but we certainly felt the power.

But power with guns is easy.

We headed home. The police still stood facing the house, staring straight ahead with self importance. We went inside, opened all the windows, and blasted drag music onto the street, and danced in the window where everyone could see.

And made more tea.

The first mouse made an appearance around then. We had a little war with that mouse, gradually wearing him down until Lulu actually caught him in a shoebox. The plan was to get it out of the house, but Lulu took one look and fell in love with it. Instead of putting him in the snow, she went two doors down to Le Marchand Mansion and let it go inside.

EVENTUALLY WE destroyed the house. Not all at once, and not on purpose. It just kind of happened.

One day the kitchen wall fell in as Trash was doing the dishes. Just peeled away and collapsed. Dozens of mice were suddenly visible running through the woodwork. A winter storm blew my bedroom window in one day. Immediately the whole upper floor plummeted to minus thirty. It was weeks before I could afford to have it fixed. Lulu threatened to move somewhere warm if I didn't do something about it. I suggested Hell and stormed out for a week.

The strain was beginning to show. Prickles started doing bizarre stuff like moving all the dirty dishes from the kitchen to the upstairs bathroom and leaving them there. Iona's mother died in BC, and suddenly Iona sank into a major depression. Trash was secretly planning to move out and go to Vancouver because she was a nomad and never really felt right owning so much stuff. Lulu was driving herself crazy meddling with the machinations of Drag Politics, and I couldn't escape the nagging feeling that there had to be more to life than chasing two-bit crowns. I wanted to make Art. And I wanted to be beautiful doing it. Lulu did her best to keep me doing comedy while she lived the role of the tragic diva.

The battle between Lulu and I for control of Edmonton's drag turf heated up after that.

The seeds of discontent had been sown. The better I got at doing drag, the more I threatened her supremacy. Lulu had moved into the unenviable position of the queen to conquer. Her hold on an audience was hard to describe—possibly it had more to do with who she was offstage, but she left crowds cheering madly.

My Mentor. My Mother.

We had ruled as a team, but when Lulu and Gloria were spoken of, Lulu's name always came first, and I was starting to get bitter.

I was no longer suited for second in line to the throne, not just comedy relief anymore. Waist length red hair made

Kevin and Gloria watch the Drag Races.

me more vain than God. I learned sultry. I studied sexy. My routines reinvented sleaze. And, I learned that I had better legs than she did.

I told you I was bitter. Remember: there can only ever be *one* queen.

Lulu and I spent weeks not speaking to each other. The bills mounted. We ignored them. We had shows to do! How dare real life intervene? Queens moved in and out and back in, the drag piled higher and higher, only now there were mice burrowing through it.

Then the sheriff arrived to seize something for nonpayment of rent, and the only thing worth taking was my piano. I called Mom in tears.

She wired me the rent. Lulu and I began making plans to move.

Then I fell in love. And nothing can tear two sisters apart faster than a man.

That was the end of Walla Walla West. We abandoned ship. In our wake, we left behind furniture, tons of newspapers, clothes that didn't fit, broken appliances, dirty dishes, an eight-foot fig tree, a statue, a headstone, and the garbage from every queen that had ever lived there.

I took one last look at the living room before I locked the front door that final time.

It was already full of ghosts.

LULU AND I moved into an apartment, but the wheels were in motion. I started making plans to move again. But I didn't tell Lulu. Right down to the day I left, we didn't speak about being apart. The words didn't exist because what we had gone through together was too unique, too manic, too special for mere words.

When I saw her at the Club the next week, we didn't mention the big move. We never did speak about it. But the Big Onion did. Queens gossiped about it for weeks, waiting for the explosion that, in spite of all the unspoken hurt, never happened.

Life went on.

That house is gone now. So are a lot of the people who lived there.

Twiggy.

Go Into The Light

1986–1987

SOMETIMES A STAR IS BORN IN SPITE OF HERSELF.

In the summer, the Big Onion explodes into four months of festivals, parties, events, and gatherings. Maybe winter in the Big Onion builds a little too much character. Maybe it has something to do with being sequestered in perpetual darkness for so many months.

Some people prefer that darkness to light, unless that light is a spotlight. Then that darkness is pierced with a dazzling ray of hope, enough to keep you drawn to its brilliance.

Twiggy was the Moth that couldn't stay away from the light.

Yet she lived in perpetual night. 4:00 AM would find her sucking back her eighth pot of coffee, chain-smoking, and doodling gown designs on a placemat at whatever all-night restaurant hadn't gone bankrupt from her patronage. She would address the graveyard shift by name, and was often still doodling and requesting refills when the changing of the guard ushered in the morning.

Twiggy would often awake just in time to make it to the Club for the peak of the evening. Her life was a constant race against the sun; the more she could squeeze into those precious hours of night, the better she would sleep when the sun finally came out.

The Underground was designed for people just like Twiggy. That's why she surprised me when she agreed to follow me to The Surface.

The reputation of The Hole Family had spread like a brush fire across the Prairies. We were now The Old Guard; there

Neon.

was no getting around it. Once the "alternative" becomes mainstream, it's only a matter of time before there's a new "alternative" waiting in the wings to dethrone it.

Tallulah's year ended with one of the largest parties Flashback had seen. She was an audience favourite from the word go; one of those performers you wanted to see succeed. When she stepped down, there was never any question as to who would be next to wear the crown: Twiggy was redefining drag movement every time she hit the stage. She was fluid, graceful, charismatic and confident. In spite of herself.

Twiggy possessed a tragic flaw: she could sleep through anything.

Many a time we would struggle to wake her up for a rehearsal. She could sleep through the phone ringing two hundred times right next to her bed. She could sleep through queens jumping up and down on her bed. She could sleep through water being poured on her head. Many times we would just give up, assuming we would have to do the show without her.

She would show up seconds before the show started, plop herself into the running order, and wow the audience. Flawlessly, as if she had been rehearsing for weeks. Never missing a step.

Ya gotta hate a queen like that.

She made every show she was in a better place to be. And as long as you didn't mind the occasional set of earrings disappearing, or your evening gloves vanishing before a performance, she could be a lot of fun, too.

Now, of course, "borrowing" things from each other was a common tool, useful when drag shortages hit. There was nothing worse than getting halfway through your face and realizing you were out of powder. Thankfully, because we all got ready together, someone else could always float you through the crisis: however, it is easier to ask for forgiveness than for permission. So, often we would merely help ourselves to each other's stashes. It was an understanding that kept us all from killing each other.

Eventually, the Club bought a set of lockers for the drag room. That settled things for a while, but anything left out in the open was communal drag property.

Twiggy's Mr. Flashback was only the second woman to possess the title, the first being a lesbian named Joey, back in the days of Millicent.

This woman was Neon, adopted into The Family when she travelled North to party for weekends, then weeks, then months at a time. Originally a member of the Calgary Del Rockos, she couldn't resist the lure of the Northern Lights, and eventually relocated permanently to the Big Onion.

Twiggy and Neon should have been Mr. and Mz. Flashback 10, because that's the number they looked like when they stood next to each other. Twiggy was named for her slight, lithe frame, while Neon became famous for impersonating all the "larger-than-life" women—Jennifer Holliday, Mama Cass, Divine—all without the aid of padded dresses.

Their reign could have been a stormy one, as both egos were larger than life. Neon, a drag queen trapped in a woman's

Twiggy.

body, had been performing with cross-dressing troupes from the second she was old enough to step foot in a fag bar; Twiggy was a Diva from the word go. Their competitive natures meant they drove each other to new heights, each vying for the lioness's share of the spotlight.

It made for a fireworks kind of year.

I broke my promise to Tallulah and gave Twiggy Entertainer of the Year.

Around then, we started exploring the surface. We were getting too numerous to stay Underground forever. The fag bar was fun, but straight people freaked when we performed for them. A few professional gigs and the occasional mention in the papers started fuelling the dream: to go pro.

After weeks of thinking carefully, I applied to the Fringe Festival to do a drag show. I chose Twiggy to write the show with me, and asked every one of the queens to come along for the ride.

Every queen but Lulu.

Maybe I had a chip on my shoulder. Maybe I resented Lulu's continuing hold on the fans. Sometimes it all seemed way too easy for her.

Maybe I just had to do it without Mom.

I remember cruising down Whyte Avenue on the hood of a '57 Pontiac in my new mermaid outfit on the opening day of the Fringe. We had transcended "freak" status and entered "local oddity" territory. Twiggy and Neon were by my side (the rest of the Girls refused to do drag that early in the day), and there was a palpable buzz of excitement in the air.

Once you go public, there's no turning back.

Guys in Disguise, 1987.

Boys Will Be Girls

August, 1987

THERE'S SOMETHING SCARY ABOUT THE SURFACE.

First, it's way too bright. Underground dwellers usually squint as they see the sunlight for the first time.

Second, people dress a lot plainer.

Lastly, people on the surface frighten easily. We figured that out quickly and turned it to our advantage.

In my wildest dreams, I never would have imagined causing anything more than a minor ripple on the surface of daylight in the Big Onion.

But this was the Fringe. And anything could happen at the Fringe.

Or, at least, that's what I had been told.

I hadn't actually been to a Fringe. Living Underground, the celebrations of summer often went unnoticed by us because of our hectic party schedule.

In the eighties, the most famous drag queen was Boy George. Divine was gaining respectability as an actor, and Ru Paul was years away from birth. The decision to go public was not one that came easily. Were the Prairies ready for the local cross-dressers to display their wares? Could Alberta face its own dark side and face the drag music? Could they accept a part of their society that the majority was terrified of admitting even existed?

Or would we get beat up?

I had no answers as I filled out the application form. All I knew was that the time felt right.

But as soon as word got out, I began to wonder.

The Underground's reaction swung between vague words of encouragement and disbelief. No one could believe that straight people would line up and pay money to see an act that most fags considered at best passé, or in the case of the militant queers, "reinforcing negative stereotypes of the gay community."

What they didn't realize was that it takes a real man to wear a dress on the prairies.

Twiggy and I would write the script, and all the girls with any talent would be in the show. That is, with the exception of Lulu.

Even as I say those words now, they seem harsh. But at the time, there was more than just friendship or sisterhood involved. Without Lulu, I could be sure that the control stayed in my hands.

I had been waiting for this all my life. But I knew that it wouldn't happen the way I wanted it to if Lulu was hanging over my head.

Twiggy, however, threw a whole new element of danger into the proceedings. Twiggy could sleep through her own funeral.

Mornings were usually spent trying to get Twiggy out of bed. I would start phoning her hours before we had to actually be anywhere. One of the most effective ways to get her out of bed was to phone, and once ringing was under way, put your own phone on hold and go get something done. Checking back every ten minutes or so, I would hear her line ring and ring and ring, then I'd go back to whatever it was I'd been doing.

Despite this, Twiggy and I wrote a play that summer. Actually, two plays. The first still languishes in my files, seventy hand-written pages of soap opera importance, with a murder, deceit, tragedy, and guilt all woven together. The first read took two and a half hours. And we still wanted to do some drag numbers.

Everyone had pretty much been cast as themselves. The cast consisted of Twiggy, Tallulah, Kim Burly, Neon, Ora, and myself. My high school friend Shanann was signed up to sing the original song. And we hired a queen wannabe, because we needed a boy for some of the numbers. His name was Nellie Michael, later to become Ginger Snapped.

The tales of rehearsals read like Macbeth. Not only were

we inexperienced, but drag queens are notorious for making a bad scene worse. I may have thought I was a writer, but I was definitely not a director. We frantically collected dresses, painted sets, hoofed our way through hour after hour of choreography. The first script was tossed; Twiggy and I began writing another.

That's when mutiny began. Queen by queen, murmurs of dissent began to filter back to my panic-stricken ears. First Ora tried to quit. She was actually running for Empress XII at the same time that all of this was happening. I pulled her aside and managed to convince her that a pro show would only enhance her campaign image. Then Kim Burly started her schizophrenic routine. She was the reigning Mz. Flashback, and my second daughter. The strains of half-truths began to unravel the already tenuous threads holding us together. Kim Burly wanted out: she'd had enough, and wanted to return to just being a bar queen. The troupe we had created was tearing apart the Family. And the Underground community lurked nearby, ready to grab tales of confusion and run them to the doubters, the few who actually wished us ill because we were dragging the dirty drag

Cleo, Gloria (de-frocked) and Tallulah, Vancouver, 1998. The Miss Gay Canada Pageant. An American queen won.

Guys Undisguised.

laundry into the sunlight where everyone could see.

Time for decisive action. I did the only thing I knew I could get away with. We had an emergency meeting, and I announced that if anyone pulled out this close to opening night, I would personally see to it that they never performed at Flashback again.

The girls looked at me. No one really believed that I could do that, but no one was willing to test that theory.

The two main dissenters, Ora and Kim Burly, shut up after that. If Ora won as Empress, she would need that stage for a whole year. And Kim Burly's hold on the Mz. Flashback crown was tenuous enough already; the management had already threatened to crown someone else if she didn't start showing up and doing something. The unique circumstances that led to this were actually fairly simple.

I had never stepped down.

Programming that stage was now my job. Ever since I had held the crown, I had supervised the grooming and coronation of the new Mz. Flashback, planned her year, did her posters, choreographed her shows, and made her look good. Tallulah had insisted on that: it was the only way we could convince her to run for the title. Twiggy and Neon had worked with me to create shows that were polished, unusual and very funny. Flashback was the drag capital of the world, according to us.

And Guys In Disguise, as we were now called, was billed as the In-House troupe of Flashback.

Around this time, we were faced with another serious discussion.

We had just finished a group photo shoot above Flashback in one of the studios that filled the rest of the building. As we piled into the freight elevator to go back downstairs, Ora said, "I want prints of those for my Empress poster."

"Girl, you'll be able to just clip it out of the paper!" I laughed. Tallulah looked at me suddenly. "Which paper?" she demanded.

"Probably the *Edmonton Journal*, maybe the *Sun*, I don't know." I didn't see the problem.

"My mom reads the *Journal*," said Ora.

"Won't she be proud when she sees you in the paper?"

Tallulah butted in. "With our real names in print?"

"Well, yeah, I mean, this is the real thing, right? We have to sell tickets. I want pictures of the whole gang in and out of costume."

"In the *Journal*?" Tallulah was getting crabby.

"What's the problem? I mean, we're queens. It's not like we live in a closet." Now I was getting crabby.

"Speak for yourself, Gloria. My whole family might see this," said Ora.

"You're running for Empress! This is not the time to be camera shy." I couldn't see the problem. "My family will see this, too. Everyone in Rocky Mountain House reads the *Journal*. But this is a legitimate theatre event. And we're artists. I want people to know who we are."

Tallulah rolled her eyes. "You mean you want people to know who *you* are."

I stared at her. "This is for all of us," I said quietly. "Don't you want to be famous?"

"We're already famous enough for me," said Kim Burly. All she had ever wanted was to be Mz. Flashback. "This stopped being about us ages ago. I don't see why we have to out ourselves just because you've got something to prove."

We took a vote. Tallulah still held back, nervous about her family in Yellowknife. Then, finally, she relented.

We did one more photo shoot: at the *Journal* building. The logistics of moving that many queens from place to place were just beginning to occur to us. It took two or three taxis, depending on how big the hair was that day. We piled out of a convoy of cabs, lamé flashing in the bright daylight. People waiting for buses stood staring as we entered the building. The eight of us strolled through the newsroom and you could have heard an eyelash drop. The photographer, dubious at first, brightened up when he saw us work the camera. We posed, minced, and giggled our way to a drop-dead gorgeous group photo.

With all this publicity to do, who had time to rehearse?

We resumed panicking. In a hideous coincidence, the Fringe was opening on Ball weekend. Not only were we opening a show on the surface for the first time, but we all had our Underground duties to fulfill as well. Ora was running for Empress, Kim Burly had a Flashback Entrance to put together, Twiggy and I each had Entertainer of the Year performances to consider. Plus, we had vowed not to use any of the numbers in our Fringe show in any other context, which meant coming up with new performances. The day of the Fringe parade, as we floated down Whyte Avenue on our way to respectability, we had already been awake for two days, buzzing on bennies to stay alert. After the parade, we took off our makeup, made coffee, sat for a couple of hours staring at nothing, then packed up our costumes and got started putting on makeup for the Ball. The whole weekend was such a blur that the impact of what we'd done barely registered.

We opened Monday. At noon.

The scheduling Gods at the Fringe obviously had it in for us. For a drag queen, a noon show means prep starts at 7:00 AM.

We sold out. No one was more surprised than us.

And the demographic of the audience surprised us: mostly straight, mostly female. We stumbled through our routines. The performance was our first real run of the whole thing. It felt like it lasted forever.

As we bowed, we received a respectable round of applause. But the show had problems.

That evening, we rebuilt the show. Top to bottom. Brand new show tapes were made. All the impersonations were cut. Tina Turner had bombed, as had my cherished Kate Bush performance. The only thing we could count on was comedy. So the whole show became about parading the shtick we had developed to entertain ourselves in the jaded Underground.

The reviews hit the next morning. Suddenly our faces were everywhere. In and out of drag. The parade had attracted a lot of attention, but nothing compared to the pre-show performances we started to give.

Our next show sold out as well. The reviews were all positive, and sales were brisk, but that didn't keep us from going for even more press. Guys In Disguise were all around you. Ora and Kim Burly did their pre-show warm-up in the actors' beer tent in full costume. Unlike most performers, drag queens don't mind being noticed in costume before a show. We would all get in drag early so we could roam the Fringe grounds for an hour before the show. Strathcona became our playground. Ora, in particular, developed a rabid taste for notoriety. She would lie down on Whyte Avenue in her beaded gown at rush hour, and the rest of us would run from car to car, sticking flyers under windshield wipers. Twiggy and I would run to the big ticket board and gloat about being sold out. We partied the entire ten days, performing and celebrating and terrorizing straight boys.

Guys In Disguise.

The head honcho of the Fringe nearly kicked us out of the beer tent for climbing over the barrier fence in tight miniskirts. We were the Big Talk in the Big Onion . . .

. . . and then we went back to our lives.

And, suddenly, the Underground seemed too dark, too closed, too rigid, too afraid of the light.

And my dragmother hated me.

And all we had were some newspaper clippings and the memory of the applause ringing in our ears . . . and a strange new sense of respect from some of the Underground.

And the *Journal* glamour photo ended up enlarged and framed and hanging at the International Airport, believe it or not. Until 1995, it was the first image of Edmonton you saw as you arrived through international customs. To this day, if we're recognized from that photo, the girls at the counter won't charge us extra for travelling with seventy-pound beaded gowns, and awkward hat boxes filled with crowns.

Shanann, Gloria, and the Journal *photo at the airport.*

Ora Fice.

Heavy Is The Wig
That Wears The Crown

IT'S HARD TO DESCRIBE THE IMPACT of a Coronation on your drag career.

The Queen you were has to be redrawn. The next year of your life has to be dedicated completely to your adoring public: the civilians who voted you in. And they have come to expect a certain standard of excellence. And you have to be that fabulous three nights a week for a whole year, with a new look, a new number, unflagging enthusiasm, superhuman fashion sense, and the liquor tolerance of a sailor on leave. All for free.

Let's see Princess Di do that. Mind you, she'll never be a Queen. Not with that wardrobe.

When your year was up, you passed the glory, willingly or not, to the new generation. Then you stepped as graciously as you could into the hallowed ranks of The Hall of Dowagers. (That's drag language for has-been.) All this meant was you were no longer in control, but the Dowagers still lurked in the vicinity, waiting for the new girl to fuck things up bad enough for them to rush in and save the day.

Lulu and I were both Dowagers when Tallulah gave birth to her first daughter, my granddaughter, Lulu's great-granddaughter:

Ora Fice.

From the very beginning, Lulu and Ora didn't see eye to eye. Ora was a strange creature: devious, ambitious, desperately seeking something. Things between Lulu and I were already strained, and the pressures of matriarchy were taking a toll. Ora merely complicated things.

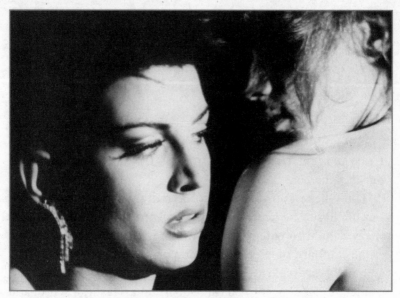

Ora and Gloria (de-frocked).

She Stoops To Conquer
1986–1987

AFTER ORA WAS CREMATED, I CARRIED HER ashes around in my car for a couple of months. Not all of her ashes, 'cause she had been divided into eight or nine "bundles." Everyone at the service got a "bundle" for themselves. I wanted to do something appropriate. But until I decided, she would just have to wait. So she stayed in the back of my car, along with some scripts, empty Diet Pepsi bottles. and the other stuff that collects if you don't clean your car regularly.

There were two services for Ora, each very different in nature. This matched her schizophrenic nature perfectly. She was simultaneously someone you had to tolerate, yet wanted to be around. Her career—a meteoric rise from drunken fag party boy obscurity to Diva Empress was a two-sided-split-personality-in-your-face-blind-ambition-tiara-at-any-cost kind of time.

Drag was taking a turn away from content and toward surface glass bead glam. The Americans were having an undue influence. Yankee Empresses had big jewellery, big lashes, big hair, big egos. Ora bought the whole philosophy and became more American than Americans.

People were tools of the trade for Ora—friends as fodder for fame—a means, not an end. If you could help make her more famous, more beautiful, or more stylish, she would keep you around. A lot.

Her boyfriend was a dress designer. How convenient. She had fresh gowns for every show. Her look was simple at first. Tall, thin, manicured, neat wig pulled back into a ponytail with a huge bow that always always always matched the dress, which was tailored, elegant, and simple. Gradually that transformed (in the post-Empress years) into forty bugle beads per square inch, earrings heavier than me, and red hair glued into a massive tidal wave sweeping over one eye.

In the early years, you could watch Ora soak up information like a makeup sponge. She would see what worked, and steal it. Intellectual property wasn't a term she really understood. She ran for Empress at an early age, but her style was still too wild, too unpredictable. She would perform a Latin number covered in real fruit which would fall off, banana by orange, turning to mush as she cavorted on stage. Or the Christmas show where she walked onto the stage decorated like a tree. The tinsel and twinkling lights looked great until she started dancing, then mayhem struck: glass balls shattering and popping as they gave up holding onto her dress, a heavy orange extension chord emerging from her crotch area, snaking across the stage and disappearing into the sound booth. Barbra Streisand's Jingle Bells will never sound the same.

Ora was the Queen of *costume interruptus*.

She lost her first bid to be Empress. She was conquered in battle by an older queen named Beverly Crest. Ora had to settle for second place in the palace for a year. That's when she became the mistress of court intrigue, blatantly manipulative, seductively scandalous, mysterious, and mischievous. Princess Power Politics became her most important talent. She waited in the wings, watching and wanting. Everyone knew she would be the next ruler.

Then along came Yoda.

I struggle for a moment to find a delicate manner of phrasing this next information, but graceful turns of tongue momentarily elude me.

Yoda was a midget drag queen.

For someone like Ora, for whom image equalled life, the remotest possibility of losing the crown she had fought so hard for to—well—a vertically challenged person was unthinkable.

Yoda shopped in the junior petite section and did Anne Murray numbers. Her humble origins as Chastity in the Sonny

& Cher performance that won me my Mz. Flashback crown had given her a new attitude. She was also becoming famous as dwarf tossing swept the bar scene.

Yoda had the advantage of a novelty vote. How many other cities could successfully hold a circus-themed drag ball? There was also the outside chance that she would get elected as a joke.

But Ora had planned for too long. Something had to be done. But what? A new proclamation: "Must be taller than this line to run for Empress"? In a secret meeting, the candidate committee ruled Yoda's application invalid.

Then, all Hell broke loose.

Since word had gotten out, Yoda had garnered more support than anyone had anticipated. Who could have known? Somehow the concept of a three and a half foot monarch didn't freak out the electorate. Lulu suddenly decided she would be the defender of Midgets' Rights. Lulu hated Ora, and all she needed was an excuse to complicate things. This was it.

So Ora watched in horror as the ranks of Yoda's supporters swelled. People even defected to the other side once the movement started to pick up momentum. Ball weekend was approaching and the numbers were dangerously close.

The candidate committee finally relented and allowed Yoda to run. Her campaign poster had a black and white picture of her standing against a white wall in her apartment,

Ora and Gloria.

Ora Fice.

trying to avoid comparisons of her height to any furniture in the room. However, the photographer didn't notice the electrical socket, low on the wall. It came up to Yoda's waistline.

Ora's performances began to feel a little desperate, like the stakes were getting higher. She would be the laughingstock of the ball circuit if all this glamour didn't sway people back to her camp. She had people coming from all over North America to witness her spectacular victory. She couldn't risk the sideshow.

The public was now viewing her as the enemy in the Dwarfgate scandal. Somehow it had all become her fault. Lulu fuelled the furor with constant reminders of the evil irresponsible things Ora had done over the years. Ora started to panic. She of the wild wicked past saw it come seeping back to haunt her.

It was time to pull out the stops. The stunts began. Ora, in a last-ditch effort, returned to her roots: insanity. She did the craziest things anyone had seen. She went into a pre-vote binge-party-week. New rumours started: Ora had been spotted on roller-skates being pulled by a station wagon down Fourth Street in a tutu in broad daylight; she rolled her mother's car and walked away from the wreck, laughing, and went back into the bar.

And the big finish: Police were called to the Palisades downtown to arrest a transvestite climbing the outside of the building, balcony by balcony—in full glamour drag. Dorky was hosting the Barbie Sacrifice party, and Ora, who lived in the same high-rise, decided on a new route to her fourteenth-floor apartment.

Opinion began to swing back. She was still the final word in glamour, but if it was a circus people wanted, she was only too willing to comply.

And somehow—it worked.

She won by a landslide and was crowned Empress XII.

Maybe it was just people coming back to their senses, or maybe something in her reckless overdressed passion struck a chord in the rest of us. To see someone desire something so badly that she would risk life and lash to climb a downtown high-rise was an inspiring sight.

Her year as Empress was the zenith of the glamour years. She set a new standard for *beaucoup de gownage*. She travelled extensively, wooing and wowing the circuit, living for the moment . . . that shining, perfect moment . . .

She had balls.

When Ora stepped down, the whole Hole Family was there. Lulu and I both did command performances, and I remember looking out at the audience from the stage and seeing what we had created . . . since we had been crowned, every

Ora.

Mz. Flashback and every Entertainer of the Year and two of the Empresses had been descendants of Lulu and me. It was like a family reunion, but with way more applause. In the snapshots from that evening, Lulu and I are surrounded by our beautiful, talented offspring. Like proud great-great-grandparents, we watched the fruits of our labours raising their own families, and we smiled.

We were immortal now. Families go on forever.

Her last night as Empress, Ora broke up with her boyfriend, the dress designer, minutes after she crowned the next Empress.

I kept all of this in mind as I drove around looking for a place to scatter the ashes. I had actually been spreading her here and there, as I saw locations that seemed significant.

Whyte Avenue and Fifth Street where she had stopped traffic in full drag in all four directions. The old Flashback alley where we had stumbled into cabs in broad daylight with beards growing through our makeup. Off a balcony at the Palisades, of course. A Greek restaurant where she had used her press-on nails to spear food off people's plates as she walked through.

Two final images . . .

At one of Ora's memorials, we went outside afterwards for a smoke. There, in the parking lot, was a car with the trunk open. Seven queens clustered around, and for a moment I couldn't figure out what they were doing. Then I saw a flash of glitter, and it looked to me like they were divvying up Ora's drag.

"Those bitches," I thought. Like vultures tearing at a beaded carcass. Devouring what she was. Ora was what she wore.

At the second memorial, I held her in my hands. Ashes are kind of like gravel. We each got a white balloon, and after speaking we let the balloons go.

Brilliant sunlight.

The white balloons floating higher and higher and further and further until they disappeared in a blur of tears, the fog of memory, like some sad, languid, beautiful dream.

Some stars burn so brightly they consume themselves.

Cleo.

All That Glitters . . .

1988

BIANCA BANG-BANG, DORKY, AND I SAT eating lunch downtown one day, when we saw a sight that made us all stop chewing our baguettes.

"Girl, look at that," chortled Bianca.

Even by our standards, the person we were watching crossed a few gender lines. It was the Michael Jackson "Thriller" jacket that caught our attention first, the mohawk second. But when we heard this young black man's voice as he ordered the soup of the day, all three of us snorted into our soup.

He sounded even more like Michael Jackson than he looked: whispery and girly, like a black Marilyn Monroe. He caught us staring at him, so we looked away quickly, not wanting to appear too rude.

"Ten bucks says we see *her* at the Club by Saturday," I said sarcastically.

Saturday arrived. And so did she.

Within a couple of months, she had stolen everyone's heart. Within a year, she was Cleo.

There's a special place in the world for people who remain eternally young, refusing all attempts at growing up . Regardless of how old she actually was, she inspired protection and motherly instincts in all of us. What at first seemed outrageously queeny gradually became endearing, then addictively funny. Her small stature and big mouth meant it was only a matter of time before we talked her into crossing the line.

For Cleo, that line was a place where you celebrated with laughter, where beauty was something you didn't take too seriously, unless it could get you free cocktails. She quickly

CLEO

MZ FLASHBACK XIII

Cleo's campaign poster.

learned the power of youth combined with beauty, then sabotaged it before it could be pinned on her as a character trait. She would work for weeks on a performance, then trash the entire thing onstage by letting her wig fly off.

The audience approved.

Cleo started out as part of a team. Much like I had found Lulu in those crucial formative years, she found her soulmate: Gracie Spoon.

The two of them, both young, black, proud, and insane, were inseparable. Together, they began the rise through the ranks of influence. But when they created comedy, the world lay laughing at their feet and begged to be put out of its misery.

Their weapon: The Lipps Sisters.

The two of them had been working on a serious drag duet for ages: "I Know Him So Well" by Whitney and Cissy Houston. For two black girls, a love duet sung by the Divas-to-end-all-Divas was a dream come true. But, as usual, Cleo started getting

Cleo (de-frocked) in the office.

cold feet before the show. She was never totally at ease with the ease of her beauty.

Minutes before showtime, Cleo changed her mind. She disappeared into the back without a word, and when she re-appeared, she had become a clown.

Gone was the immaculate Supremes hair: she had teased it impossibly high and decorated it with cocktail umbrellas. Gone was the stunning evening gown: she had replaced it with a Value Village muumuu from the drag pit.

And gone was the perfect makeup she had spent hours fussing over: Cleo had repainted her lips so that they took over her face.

Clown with no conscience.

When Gracie spotted her, she shrieked.

The show was only minutes away. It was too late to do anything but follow suit.

Gracie swallowed her pride and conformed.

When The Lipps Sisters hit the stage, camp met crazy and a Drag Classic was born. The Lipps Sisters were an overnight sensation, leaving trails of polyester-lined hilarity wherever they performed. Cleo and Gracie became the new toast of the Big Onion.

It was only a matter of time before they began to hunger for the crown.

Much like Lulu and I, Gracie and Cleo lived together, performed and partied together, laughed and cried together. Also like Lulu and I, Gracie wanted to be Empress and Cleo coveted the Mz. Flashback crown.

They took over the scene within months.

That's when envy reared its ugly green head.

Cleo's love of life, laughter, and the pursuit of fabulous hair didn't exactly mesh with Gracie's ambitions. She gradually saw the spotlight favouring Cleo, the way attention is showered on a favourite child. Bit by bit, friendship evaporated into a good-natured rivalry, then collided head-on with out-and-out jealousy. Gracie was definitely the boss, but her little sister was hungrily lapping up all the praise and adoration that the mob had to offer.

By this time, both had been adopted into the Family: Gracie as my foster daughter, and Cleo as Tallulah's foster daughter. There was room for everyone, or so we thought.

When Ora stepped down as Empress, Gracie was the favoured candidate to win. While she waited in the wings for the new ruler to be announced, Cleo was already the new Mz. Flashback. And, as always, the audience breathlessly awaited the Flashback entrance.

We had been working for weeks on the performance. Cleo would be "Christine" in "Phantom," hauled into the Ballroom by slaves pulling a huge gondola on wheels. She would glide up to the dais, dismount, and wow the crowd with her beauty and poise.

Or, at least, that was the plan.

The gondola was a work of art. Seven feet high, with a curved, Viking-like front. Constructed by the cranky-but-lovable punk

anarchist club carpenter Mr. Dick, it glided effortlessly in all the test runs, even with a queen on board. The whole affair was sprayed with a clear adhesive, and then covered in red glitter. It caught the light magically, like a glitzy Loch Ness monster. I could picture the reaction as it floated through the ballroom.

There was only one problem: the glue wouldn't dry.

That was fine, we thought, as there was still a week until the ball.

A week later, the glue still hadn't dried. You couldn't touch the gondola without your hand coming away covered in red glitter. "Don't touch the gondola!" Cleo would scream at anyone who was admiring it. And we still had to figure out how to get it to the hotel for the Ball, let alone how to drag it up to the dais without getting glittered to death.

So we assigned the task of transporting it to two butch staff members, while we packed up our costumes and headed to the Ball. We were behind schedule, but that was par for the course; Drag Time meant we were probably right on time.

As we entered the Ballroom, we realized that for the first time in history, the Ball had actually started on time. Ora, trying to prove some point about her organizational skills, had insisted that the time posted was the actual time it would start. This threw the entire evening into a panic. As we stood there with Cleo, scanning the Ballroom for our reserved Flashback table, we heard:

"Ladies and gentlemen, the Reigning Mz. Flashback, Cleo!"

We looked at each other in disbelief as the "Phantom" music started. We had just entered the room! We were nowhere near ready. Neon screamed "Cut the music!" and headed to the emcee to plead for more time, as we frantically searched the badly lit backstage for our costumes, swearing, pushing queens out of our way as we emptied bags onto the floor.

Of course, we had forgotten all the robes for the slaves. In fact, the only ones who had remembered their costumes were Cleo and her Mr. Flashback, Zola.

"Here, wear this," shouted Neon as she threw whatever she could find at all the backup. We would just have to make do. We draped fabric around us, trying to make it look like a style choice. We were ready to completely make up the whole entrance.

But the gondola finally arrived as we stood in the wings, ready to go on.

We were saved! We lifted Cleo into the gondola. Immediately, her five hundred dollar gown received a shock of red glitter up the backside. "Don't touch the gondola!" she screamed, frantically trying to brush it off. The wet glue just smeared, spreading the glitter to her hands.

We stood, stoic, serious, and waited for the music to start. Zola took his place on the ramp, wearing his Phantom mask. The first organ chords flew through the air.

We took a deep breath and began pulling the gondola into the Ballroom. The crowd cheered, recognizing the music immediately, as they always did.

The walk leading up to the dais was about forty feet long, and covered in red carpet for that pseudo-regal feel. *This will be fabulous,* I thought, picturing how we must look as we floated into view.

Then the gondola stopped short, with a mighty jerk that almost threw Cleo onto the floor.

The red carpet had bunched up under the wheels and frozen it in place.

The slaves tugged, trying to get past the sticking point. They succeeded, almost knocking Cleo over again in the process. Then five feet later, it happened again. This time, however, the carpet was so piled, the slaves couldn't budge it. They looked up at Cleo, wondering what to do next. One of them went to grab the sides to push. "DON'T TOUCH THE GONDOLA!" screamed Cleo.

Finally, exasperated past the point of politeness, Cleo rolled her eyes. "FUCK IT!" she exclaimed, loud enough that it was audible over the blaring Lloyd Webber. She hoisted up the voluminous skirts of her five hundred dollar gown, climbed out of the gondola, marched up to the dais, and finished her number.

The crowd clapped politely, but we all knew the Entrance had been ruined.

Flashback won the Best Entrance award that night, but it was obviously out of sheer pity. The gondola ended up in the dumpster outside Flashback the next day.

A week later, before the garbage truck picked up the refuse, I went and touched the gondola.

The glue had finally dried.

Gracie became the new Empress, then started her own drag family.

Lulu and I immediately banished her for her betrayal.

Gloria.

Cry Me A River

1990

TALLULAH'S REIGN ENDED TRIUMPHANTLY, and gave way to the sophistication of Twiggy. Twiggy passed the crown to Kim Burly, my second daughter. The thirteenth Mz. Flashback was Cleo, spawn of Tallulah, and Ora's foster sister, who bequeathed the title to Gretchen Wilder, Ora's insane daughter. The last year of the Dynasty was 1990. Christine, a very convincing sex change, beat all the drag competition and became the first transgender crowned in the Big Onion. She didn't last the year, however. Partway through the year, she resigned and gave the crown to Leah Weigh. Leah decided she would rather be Empress, however, and bequeathed the title to Ginger Snapped, who moved to Florida to become a big

drag star. She left the crown in the care of Mandy Kamp, Ora's Princess and eldest daughter. Mandy was the last Mz. Flashback.

She never stepped down. There was no Flashback by the time the year was up.

The glass brick wall was dismantled and moved out in the middle of the night. Pieces of it, and the rest of the Club, moved to garages and basements all over the city.

When Flashback closed its doors, an era of Edmonton's

The Razzberries (Ginger Snot, Lindee Star and Mrs. K.) and Gloria, 1987.

The very last Mr. and Mz. Flashback party, May 23, 1989. This was also the last time we were all together while everyone was still alive. Back row: Nellie Michael, Zola, Dorky, Twiggy, Tallulah, Gloria. Centre row: Bianca Bang-Bang, Cleo, Neon, Mr. K. Front row: Trash, Millie, Gretchen.

Underground history was officially over. The scene still exists, but no longer boasts the shining jewel of the Prairies. The evil landlords evicted the Family so they could turn the warehouse into condos.

By the time it happened, Lulu had been gone a couple of years, which was just as well. She didn't have to see what happened. She didn't have to watch our lives get hauled to the dumpster, or see the rage as the staff, evicted from their Home, kicked in walls and broke windows.

She had gone to Toronto to do a pro show. She never came back.

And the Family, with no Matriarch and no Home, drifted around the world and lost contact. With no escape from reality, we faced the light and started our new lives.

Our time together in the Big Onion ended pretty silently for two people as loud as Lulu and I were. We drifted like ice floes for a time, bumping off each other, sometimes connecting, often missing. Egos had been bruised, feelings hurt, things said . . .

The Club that ate Edmonton slipped away and sank under the water: the Titanic of fag bars. We had all assumed she was unsinkable, that she would float forever, taking us to warmer places, but taking us.

Our lives, like lifeboats left after a disaster, seemed awfully small for a while. And lonely.

And the body count hadn't even started yet.

Gloria in the Edmonton City Hall reflecting pool, 1996.

A Fish Out Of Water

August 1994
Downtown Edmonton

FESTIVAL CITY. OR, AT LEAST, THAT'S WHAT we call it. Some misguided civic politician decided, at some point, to nickname the Big Onion "The City of Champions".

Then Gretzky was traded to LA and the local team stopped winning.

Someone should have told that politician not to brag. Trophies mean little once they've moved on. But the mentality of the men who run this province has always been dubious, to say the least. They decided that "champions" were what this city was most famous for, and erected a large sign on the outskirts proudly proclaiming that fact.

The trophy never came home again.

Years ago, Lulu and I had decided that what they probably meant was "City Of Champignons", but not wanting to spark up a heated bilingual debate, we let it go.

What the Big Onion is truly remarkable for is its dynamic summer festival season. Starting in June, the locals could consecutively view world-class jazz, visual arts, folk music, theatre, even street performers.

I watched Sir Winston Churchill Square that summer as it throbbed with families. The true heart of downtown, it was the home of many celebrations. City Hall presided over the proceedings with a stately air. Next to it stood that clock tower where my ill-fated New Year's Eve go-go experience had happened. But it would be different this time.

For one thing, it wasn't minus forty degrees outside.

Actually, it was blisteringly hot. Big Onion summers are a thing to behold: hour after endless hour of sunlight so bright it hurts. Especially at noon when shadows shrunk to nothing and there was no escape from the heat.

Being in drag in heat like that presents as many problems as cranking in mid-winter. Makeup melts at thirty degrees.

It was thirty-five above, and I was once again beginning to question my judgment. As always, the concept had sounded good on paper.

Ever since that first Fringe parade, my mermaid costume had become a camera magnet. Pull the tail on, and watch the fun begin. I had been photographed in it enough times that it had become a very recognizable image. And with the release of Disney's "The Little Mermaid," it seemed like an even better idea to dig the old fish tail out of the mothballs and give it a run. My mermaid tail was exactly the same shade of aquamarine as Disney's, even though mine had been constructed three years earlier. It had gotten me onto the front page of the *Journal* two summers in a row.

It was not without its problems, however. Once the tail was on, movement was next to impossible, unless you were a champion hopper. It consisted of a foam tail that your feet slipped into, then a spandex tube that pulled up like one leg of a giant pair of pantyhose. A matching bikini top with built-in foamies, pulled on over the head like a T-shirt, was placed over the nipples. It was notorious for slipping and revealing at crucially public times.

It was also an outfit in which a tuck was of paramount importance. Spandex is the single most merciless fabric when it comes to what you're trying to hide underneath it. The practicalities of this complex ritual is one I've been steering to avoid, but it is unique to the art form, and deserves at least a brief passage of explanation.

A "tuck" is the process of removing penile evidence in the crotch area, usually only important in tight, revealing outfits. It is generally performed with a dance belt, but a good queen should be able to tuck with a roll of duct tape and a rubber band. Lulu used to refer to the process as being remarkably similar to GLAD sandwich bags: flip, flop, fold the top. Let's just say you're sitting on your own testicles all night.

And the only thing in the world that hurts more than being in tuck is taking it out at the end of the night.

But I digress.

This was the plan:

Meet the Street Performer staff boy at the info booth with a ladder. My shift starts at noon. I arrive in a long coat, to hide the fact that I'm wearing only a tiny aquamarine Speedo as a foundation garment. (Mother used to say: "What if you're in a car accident in drag and your underwear isn't colour-coordinated?") Ladder-boy and I rendezvous at the information booth. He looks at me oddly. I remember that I have a full face of makeup and a long red wig on. But I'm also in bare feet, because you can't have footwear with a mermaid tail. My tail is in a green garbage bag by my side. He leans the ladder against the aluminum booth and I scamper up to the roof, garbage bag in tow.

As soon as I'm on the roof, I see the ladder pulling away. Some high wire jugglers need it for their show, and it'll be back at the end of my shift: two o'clock. I sit, trying to figure out how to deal with delicately dressing in full sunlight on a hot tin roof in a park filled with packs of daycare field trips, the main audience at that early hour. I decide that if I just do it efficiently and quickly, it won't attract much attention.

With my back to the park and my legs dangling over the edge of the info booth, I slip my feet into the foam tail and pull up the aquamarine spandex tube. In order to get it all the way on, however, I have to do the tail-in-the-air routine, flipping it around as I stretch the fabric up. Finally, it's ready. I pull on the bra-piece, spin it around until the foam covers my nipples, and voila! I'm ready. Thank God I had the good sense to tuck in the change room. But just in case I pop my tuck, I at least had the resource to drag along some large pieces of purple and pink chiffon, long enough to drape over my midsection and drape to the ground, flowing in the slight breeze.

I grab my harp, and face the square.

Five minutes later, I'm already not having fun. The July sun rains down like lava, melting everything in its path. The concept of a fish on a hot tin roof that just kept getting hotter hadn't occurred to me. I have to keep shifting positions to keep from burning, and with my legs locked together in the spandex tube, there are only so many comfortable poses. I switch every time the heat becomes unbearable, repositioning the chiffon strategically, holding the harp at different angles.

My high vantage point provides me with a unique view of the park. The lunch rush is in full swing, with suits and ties and power dresses and bag lunches in view everywhere. Many people are being tormented by clowns or musicians or sundry characters. The fun thing about the street performer's life is tormenting the civilians, an echo of my former freedom Underground. The ones in disguise always have an advantage. Street performing has an edge of the dangerous built into the job.

The rest of the square's inhabitants are children, hundreds of them. The paltry few daycare supervisors run around like dogs, herding the kids into barely manageable circles. Their attention is diverted easily, and they move from tightrope to balloon art to sword swallowing rapidly. I am grateful for this, as my act is little more than a visual punchline. I sit, posed, on the roof.

Most of the kids can't even see that high. I'm way out of their field of vision.

I have a couple of interactions with some children. One thing you learn quickly about kids is that they're never afraid to ask the questions the adults will only wonder silently about. A little boy comes running up, thinking I am Ariel of Disney fame. "Look, Mommy! The mermaid!" The words are barely out of his mouth when he stops himself. His mouth drops open with disbelief. "That's a guy!" His mother is confused; she has no framework for dealing with this. She drags him away, both of them looking back suspiciously.

A *Journal* photographer approaches. Lulu trained me to smell a photo opportunity at seventy paces. I launch into the repertoire: harp in the air, then tail up, arch wiggle wiggle, chiffon floating in the breeze, the wind beneath my wig. I am the siren, luring unsuspecting sailor boys starved for a different kind of fish, my song of seduction dragging them to their watery graves, their souls forfeited in a deadly game with only one outcome. As the reporter clicks madly, and I make love to the camera, I hear a decidedly youthful voice. It carries a note of childhood skepticism, and its sense of logic has conviction.

"Real mermaids can't get on roofs."

I look down at a small boy. He watches me closely, ice cream cone in hand. "How come you're not in the water?" he asks, gesturing to the City Hall reflecting pool.

"Are you kidding? In this outfit, I'd drown. Do you know how much foam I'm wearing?" Some grown-ups laugh, but my humour is lost on the boy.

"You're a boy. Mermaids can't be boys. You're not a mermaid." He stands and says this calmly, but definitively.

I suddenly realize that in all my hours and hours of routines and comebacks and insults for controlling hostile situations, there is absolutely nothing in my arsenal for dealing with kids. I could probably deal with a drunk bunch of horny sailors better than I could hold my own with this boy's determined questions. He continues.

"I just saw your boy-tit!" he giggles. "You're a boy. You can't dress like a mermaid."

Suddenly a gaggle of daycare four-year-olds surrounds him. A lone woman watches the whole pack, barely maintaining control. Two little girls start with more probing questions. "How did you get up there with no legs?" "How come you're out of the water and you're not dead?" "Why are you dressed like a girl? Boys don't wear makeup." "You're not a mermaid. You are a man!"

The little boy picks up the chant. Then all the kids. *You are a ma-an, you are a ma-an, . . .* if I just ignore them they'll stop . . . *you are a ma-an, you are a ma-an, you are a ma-an, you are a ma-an, you are a ma-an, you are a ma-an, you are a ma-an, you are a ma-an, you are a ma-an, you are a ma-an . . .* this can't go on much longer . . . *you are a ma-an, you are a ma-an, you are a ma-an, you are a ma-an, you are a ma-an, you are a ma-an . . .* why doesn't that stupid bitch teacher get them away from me . . . *you are a ma-an, you are a ma-an, you are a ma-an, you are a ma-an, you are a ma-an, you are a ma-an, you are a ma-an, you are a ma-an, you are a ma-an, you are a ma-an, you are a ma-an . . .*

For the next hour, every time they were within view, they would pick up the chant again.

I could hear them as they moved around the square. I lay there, eyes gazing up at the sun. Participation in the surroundings

seemed pointless. I ignored everything, said nothing, just flapped my tail sadly if anyone talked to me.

Even at that tender age, the lines in the sandbox are so clearly drawn that those kids refused to allow me to cross over. They attacked me because they were already afraid of challenges to the divided: the boy-girl world. They were already afraid of someone who refused to be one. Or the other.

I had forgotten that the price for being on land is your voice.

Or at least, it is for mermaids.

Gloria.

The Truth About Fried Eggs

'Cause the truth about fried eggs, see . . .
is you can call it a fried egg; you can call it anything you want.
But everybody's got one.
Some people wear them on the inside,
and some people, they wear them on the outside.
—Bette Midler, Live At Last

PEOPLE SOMETIMES ASK HOW AN OTHERWISE reasonable young man could turn his back on everything and dive Underground. What makes a person pull out of the world of men and women and strike out on his own, reinventing Gender like it was something to be shed at the earliest possible convenience, laughing in the faces of the people most baffled by it, throwing their pain and confusion into full view where it was most visible.

The truth is, for most of these men, that they were never whole until they made peace with the very part of themselves that society damned. They all looked in the mirror early in life and tried to figure out why they seemed so unusual. What did people see that made them so dangerous, the target of abuse and mockery? When they finally looked into the looking glass and saw her, the woman they had been avoiding all their lives, the one inside, every motherly instinct of protection sprung into action. Suddenly they had someone to protect. Suddenly they all became valuable. To themselves.

Suddenly someone mattered.

There isn't a more public therapy on the market. There are no how-to books. You learn the art from the artists themselves. Your personal growth happens onstage and in the public eye and in glamour photo shoots.

Twiggy, Mandy and Kim Burly, Guys in Disguise, 1993.

Under the ostrich-feather wing of your sister-mother-goddess figure, the real world disappears. All the garbage you're fed about being a man is revealed for what it is: control.

Because if you don't control men, there is the chance that they may figure it out. They may see through the dogma-infested fear mongering paranoia that is life in the twentieth century and realize: it's all a lie.

The man they want you to be doesn't exist. He has to be created. By Men.

Men are controlled by Men's controls. Defending their power, they become controlled by it. And the men they can't control are exiled.

Out of sight, out of mind.

But some men refuse to stay out of sight. Crossing the line of control takes the very elements that terrify men and dresses them up and shoves them straight back in their crotches.

Every time a red-blooded hetero boy is attracted, even for a split second, to that strange Amazon on the dance floor, what is he responding to? Femaleness? Hardly. More like the trappings.

His blood stirs in response to the stuff we put on: the big tits, the impossible curves, the come-fuck-me attitude, the unnatural padding, the torturous shoes . . .

He responds to all the stuff women have spent decades discarding in their quest for equal footing.

He responds to a woman created completely by another man, using all the repressive techniques men have wished upon women to turn them into fantasy objects, most of which were invented by men.

The men that crossed the line reached a new stage of evolution—whether they knew it or not. By casting off the man they became more human.

Drag says a lot more about men than it does about women. That's why it hurts so much when some women say drag is misogynistic. On the contrary; it's the most feminist thing a man can do.

There's nothing like walking in someone else's shoes for discovering how much they hurt.

Gloria and Tallulah.

I'll Be Seeing You . . .
1990–1997

HAPPILY EVER AFTER . . .

Isn't that how all fairy tales end?

This already feels like a lifetime away . . .

All I have to do is remember.

Like I could ever forget.

What sounds like generations was a few years.

Each of us got the same prize, although the methods differed.

We arrived in Edmonton with no family. So we built one.

The only roots we knew were some two-bit hairdresser's mistake, yet we took root and flourished.

All of these men had one thing in common. They were willing to put themselves on hold, sometimes for up to a decade or more, while their own bodies and souls became a means of expression. Their own personalities and maleness stepped gracefully aside to give the inner woman free reign.

It was a life of Pumps and Circumstance. Rather than hide their pain, they strapped it on and accessorized it. Wear your shame and make it look better than God ever intended.

They became living, walking, breathing, screaming, chain-smoking Art. A live canvas ready to be tweezed, shaved, waxed, plucked, painted, glued, beaded, teased, sprayed, and ultimately displayed.

Then, like all art, viewed, perused, mocked, scorned, criticized, adored, ignored. In trying to set themselves apart, they become part of the drag / fag landscape: glitzy scenery that you always see but rarely acknowledge.

Even Underground, there are those who say that drag is

about covering up what you really are.

On the contrary: nothing could be more revealing. Drag showed us who we were.

Yet I know surprisingly little about the previous lives of these creatures. Much of that has vanished with them, as if they didn't really exist until they disappeared Underground. Their first act as adults was to reinvent themselves; the name they grew up with was shed immediately, and in its place a new human was born, free of the shackles and fear that characterized their early years. I was surprised as I wrote this to realize that I knew absolutely nothing about how Lulu ended up in Edmonton. A few phone calls later, and I realized that only Lulu has that story. There was much about our lives that we shared; there were volumes more that we didn't. I know that she was an army brat, and lived in Germany, Nova Scotia, and Innisfail, but not much more. I know that Tallulah came out to her mother while she took a bath. Tallulah sat on the toilet seat and told her naked mother "I'm gay." Her mother replied, "Don't tell your father." But not much more.

I know that Ora was predeceased by her brother, while her insane alcoholic father languished in a mental home, dying soon after, and then her mother, who I had met at the Drag Races, passed away after a long battle with heart disease. But not much more.

We went Underground to hide from ourselves. Instead, we discovered ourselves.

In every world, there are two universes: the one you see, and the one you refuse to see.

A decade has now passed since Guys In Disguise first appeared on the surface. At the time, it seemed no more than a chance to do a show and make some cash doing what we loved doing. It took me years to realize that it was a crucial period in all of our development, a tiny act of defiance that changed every one of us forever.

You don't change the world by doing what it tells you to do.

The world has gone through some big changes. So much has

happened in that decade.

Tallulah died in 1993. It had been two years since we had spoken. Like most mothers and daughters, we were never great about keeping in touch. Our last visit was chock full of the all-night marathon talks for which she was so famous. She climbed on her Italian soapbox a few times, telling me off, telling off the world but I was the only one there. It didn't matter as long as someone could hear.

She told me about getting full vision for the first time in her life in her twenties. She got goosebumps describing the shade of blue of the surgeon's uniform as he peeled the bandages from her eyes.

It was the first colour other than black that she had seen in years.

I had heard the story before, but I cried anyway.

Then she asked why I was the only one who didn't cry when she told me she was going to die.

I still don't have an answer for that one.

Her last reign was as Imperial Princess to Moira in Vancouver. In her step-down

Tallulah.

Lou.

Iona Box and Lulu in the drag pit.

message, she took her last brutally honest jab at everyone in her life. To her daughter Ora, a haunting riddle: *It's too bad you never reached out for the help you obviously needed.*

She died surrounded by family. Her Old World mother, speaking no English but understanding all, was by her bedside.

Excretia died in Toronto. She just kind of disappeared from our lives. She spent her last days in the care of her mother. The image of an ordinary Maritime woman looking after the skinhead drag queen who had terrorized the Big Onion so many years before is a striking one.

One of Iona's poems was published in the first edition of an award winning play. The award came after she, too, had returned to the Okanagan to die with her family present.

At some point, the Family we had created stopped being enough. Dragmothers faded in the picture as real mothers re-entered the drama. To care for their boys.

Priorities change when your children are threatened.

Ironically, the very thing that distanced these boys from their families drew them back together for one final time. Life is to be valued, regardless of how it is lived. Time became precious as these mothers struggled to match the son they knew with the film noir movie star photos on the wall and the tiaras in the trophy case: a sudden desperate need to understand while it mattered, while it could still make a difference.

The value of life skyrocketed.

In a cruel twist of fate, Ora became an orphan again when Tallulah went to that Spotlight in the Sky. Ora stood alone.

She died two springs ago. I got the message on my answering machine. She had been dead a few days when they found her on her living room floor. All her furniture was piled up against the door to the apartment.

Who knows what she was trying to keep out.

Two long-lost aunts emerged from the woodwork to fight over the insurance money. Her gowns were sold in the parking lot at the funeral home to pay for the service. We were the only real family there.

Millie left this world in 1996, twenty years after she began the system that would dominate our lives for so many years. The partying finally did her in. She was found in her room on skid row. Her body disappeared for a while before the funeral, in an eerie Marilyn Monroe-type mystery, but was recovered just in time. Two decades after she first laid the groundwork for an alternative universe, the system lives on. And on.

When Ginger Snot died . . .
When Prickles died . . .
When Lori St. John died . . .
When Yoda died . . .
When Zola died . . .
When Reena died . . .
When Mother Jean died . . .
When Joeboy died . . .
When Grandma Kerr died . . .
When Bianca Bang-Bang died . . .

Trash next to one of his sculptures . . . sticks and stones . . .

A news camera crew caught up with Trash in Vancouver. For years, massive stone art was appearing around the sea wall overlooking English Bay. No one could explain these free-standing feats of balance; rumours abounded as to who was building them and what they meant. Finally, a work-in-progress was captured on film: there was Trash, more mature but still wiry and muscular, hoisting rocks and driftwood twice his own weight and free-balancing them repeatedly until they stayed in place through sheer willpower. As always, Trash rearranged landscape until it suited his mood. The giant sculptures, constructed out of the refuse of the sea, stood silhouetted against the sunset, silently keeping watch over the spot in the bay where his brother's ashes were scattered.

As usual, Trash took no credit until forced to. Art for him was like breathing: it just happened while you lived.

Lulu lives in Halifax. God help the East coast. I hear she's taken the town by storm. No surprise: Lulu cornered the market on charisma years ago. She presides over the Atlantic like a Zen Mother, spawning Holes with abandon, creating rich histories,

Gloria and Trash behind the bar.

family ties that, for a moment, bind together the Outcast Elite, the Lucky ones that get to see it all. Under her great wings the real world disappears.

Tina, Mandy, Mrs. K., and Cleo reside on the West coast. Kim Burly finally moved to Calgary, where Lindee Star also lives. Twiggy, Neon, and Gretchen still terrorize Edmonton, only now they're the Old Guard.

I stood on the High Level Bridge and opened the last of Ora's ashes. She scattered in the wind, falling into the river, disappearing into the murky flow. The water was brown, not blue. It's the same river, but older. It carries more within itself.

My Girls.

They knew how to live. Then they learned how to die.

Robbed of years of majesty, decades of potential.

Most of them didn't reach thirty.

It's easy to forget that all of these people are men. We were all "she's" back then. I still call them that. Respect for the art they created, the art they embodied.

The drag they wore was no different than the drag every

Lulu and one of her Halifax drag daughters, Jay Wells, Peggy's Cove.

human dons every day of his / her life, every time he / she is presenting anything other than what they actually are. Drag may be a disguise, but it's also an illumination. It clearly tells people how you want to be perceived.

That being said, even if I never wear another dress as long as I live, I remain, and will always be, a Queen.

We all were. Are.

So here's to Men like us.

We came from farms and cities and fishing villages and oil rig towns and dysfunctional families and well-adjusted families and ministers' families. We are your hairdressers, your bank tellers, your mailmen, your teachers, your brothers, your sons, that hot guy that moved in next door.

We lived among you.

We lived with abandon.

We lived here, in spite of the rules, in spite of ourselves.

We lived fast and hard and dangerous lives, and most of you never noticed.

We lived.

All we had in common was an age-old awareness that somehow we were different at the very core.

This isn't about not being good at hockey.

It's about knowing from the word go that in a world of men and women, you are neither.

And both.

Their names are all now legend Underground. The land they ruled over churns on and on without them. You can't stop time. Crowns get passed around like rhinestone cookie cutters. Prizes for being the most . . . whatever it is at the moment.

But here on earth, there's just big empty spaces where they used to be.

Every time I hear one of their old drag numbers, a snapshot pops into view—sculpted hair, lips quivering, arms stretched out at the stand-up mic, the brilliant spotlight cascading down, then breaking like a million mirrors, refracted by jewels into shattering beams until we were blinded, their eyes gazing upward, sparkling with life and emotion and passion for their separateness, their existence, that moment, like their whole life culminated on that stage in that moment, that shining, perfect moment . . .

The Applause.

The Lucky Ones.

Everyone should feel that before they die.

" . . . and did I ever tell you
that when I was little
I would stand under a street lamp
and pretend
that I
was a beam
of light?"
—Stephen Dyson AKA Iona Box

Gloria, Lulu and Justine on the Chaps/Badlands float,
Toronto Gay Pride Parade, 1991-ish.

The Queen's English

(A Lip Glossary)

amateur night	Halloween.
Anchor	The best number in a show. Usually the last, and usually featuring the reigning monarch.
Ball	A yearly gathering of queens, bidding the previous dynasty farewell, and crowning the new Monarchs.
Barbies	Blond female heterosexuals.
Barry T's wannabes	Straight people who go to fag bars because they're more fun and the music is better.
the Big Onion	Edmonton, Alberta.
the Big Shave	Face, chest, armpits and stomach. Never legs, if you can help it. That's what multiple layers of pantyhose are for.
black bathing suit	A mythic piece of clothing that Lulu searched for over four years, every time she did drag. Its actual existence has never been verified, but, according to her, it formed the foundation for everything she had planned on wearing.
boing-boing-turn-around	How Barbies dance.
"borrowing"	Wearing something without asking the permission of the queen to whom it belongs.

Breast	Anything used to stuff a bra. Possibilities include foamies, nylons filled with rice or popcorn (unpopped), balloons, water balloons, toilet paper, or socks (that way, you know where they are when you get out of drag).
Breeders	Heterosexuals.
Chomp	An expression to show appreciation for a studly male specimen.
the Circuit	The tour of North America's Ball schedule.
cocksucker red	The perfect shade of lipstick.
come-fuck-me pumps	An essential wardrobe item.
cookie cutter	Crown.
costume interruptus	Something falling off as you perform.
Cowtown	Calgary, Alberta.
Crank	To do drag.
Derelicts	Young, cute, "straight" boys that the management bribes with liquor to pretty up the place in the hope that they will eventually put out.
Dowager	A queen who has stepped down. Also referred to as "Dogwagger."
drag hag	A straight girl who prefers the company of queens.
drag pit	The dressing room / costume storage.
drag time	One or two hours later than the actual time posted.
eating dead babies	Getting caught with lipstick on your teeth.

elected boy titles	The man on your arm while you have a crown. Sometimes an equal partner, sometimes a glorified escort.
Embarassment of Bitches	A group of Queens around a table (similar to a pride of lions or a murder of crows).
Empress	A title given to the queen who wins the most votes at the Ball. She then represents the city's drag community for a year.
Empress damage	The ego alteration that occurs after you've possessed a crown. *See also: glitzworm.*
fag hag	A straight girl who wants to sleep with fags.
Fish	A derogatory term for female.
Flashback	A private gay bar, where drag queens ruled from 1976 to 1991.
The Foxy Lady	The bar next door to Flashback. The name says it all. On average, three ambulances a week would arrive to deal with the wounded.
fruit fly	A straight girl who prefers partying with fags.
genderfuck drag	Part of the punk movement. Androgyny with a touch of S&M thrown in.
the Girls	Whoever you were out with in drag.
Glamazon	A glammed-out Queen who towers over six feet before the heels.
the glitzworm	The bug. Legend claimed that the glitzworm lived in the drag pit, disguised with pieces of discarded sequins, feathers, or tinsel. While you were sitting at the head mirror,

the glitzworm would sneak up to you (invisible because of its camouflage) and insert a long, hollow tongue in your ear and inject your brain with a poison that made you think you were always onstage and always beautiful. There is no known antidote. *See also: Empress damage.*

Gorillapause	Hairy hands.
great moments in spork	An embarrassing drag moment caught on film or video (i.e. popping a tuck onstage, passing out in drag, giving head in the handicapped stall in the ladies' can, etc.).
green	The spotlight colour you shine on queens you hate.
Harem	The group of girls, ex-girlfriends, and wives of straight disc jockeys.
the hassle team	A group of queens that follow the beat cops through the Club distracting and harassing them.
high drag	Beaded gowns, tiaras and piled hair.
the Hill	Where teenage hustler boys work. Particularly busy just after last call.
Husbands	The police.
Jasper Avenue	The Big Onion's main street.
Klondike Days	A Big Onion event (for straight people) at which the whole city is forced to wear outfits even a queen would eschew.
Kool-Aid lips	Leftover lipstick that won't come off the day after.
little black dress	An essential wardrobe item.
low drag	Anything that's not high drag.

Mary, Margot, Sister, Girlah	Terms of endearment. Can be applied to any queen.
message number	A slow drag number chosen because the lyrics hold a "message" for a friend. Usually a good time to head to the bar for a shooter.
Myrna fish drag	Trying to look like a real woman.
Mz. Flashback	The elected head of Flashback's drag stage for a year.
new guard	The queens who want the crowns.
off the street	Resigning from hooking. Notice it's not called "going straight."
old guard	The queens who have the crowns.
one-size-fits-all	An evil lie.
Paint	To apply makeup.
Panstick	Roll-out pancake base. SHAME on MAX FACTOR for discontinuing their panstick in Canada, leaving thousands of Queens without decent foundation.
pop a tuck	A good luck wish before you go onstage (the drag equivalent of "break a leg"). *See also:* **tuck**.
prairie fairy	A fag from Alberta, Saskatchewan, or Manitoba.
Princess	A title given by the Empress to the queen she wants for her second in command (usually her best friend). Update: Princess is now an elected title.
Purple City	Age-old Big Onion party ritual (even straight people do this one). Hang out at the Legislature, stare into the floodlights, and then look at the

	skyline. Everything appears purple. No one is sure how this originated, but everybody's done it.
raccoon eyes	Leftover mascara that won't come off the day after.
the Razzberries	Mrs. K., Lindee Star, and Ginger Snot.
Reverend Bob	The ex-minister who worked the front door.
rhinestone turkey baster	A fabulous stage microphone.
screaming section	Wherever Lulu and I would sit in a late night restaurant.
smell her	A dismissive insult that can be applied to either gender.
the Strip	Where the hookers (not all of them real women) work.
tough drag	Full glamour drag, but with full facial hair, or hairy chest in a strapless gown. The day after the Ball, all the men with elected boy titles have to do tough drag. Officially, it's so they can feel what it's like to be in drag all the time, but really it's just for us girls to laugh at them for a change.
Tranny	Originally a term for transsexuals, it eventually became an all-encompassing word for any queen.
Transgender	Anyone who is anywhere along the scale between man and woman.
Tuck	The process of hiding the penis in a skimpy outfit.
tundra Fairy	A fag from Canada's North.
Underground	The gay scene.

Value Village   Where a thrifty queen shops. Used dresses, antique costume jewellery, and platform shoes at rock-bottom prices. Best for skinny queens with small feet. Bitches.

wicked web   The web of nylon between the cotton gusset in the crotch of your pantyhose and your actual crotch. Usually only a concern for tall queens. *See also: **Glamazon**.*

work the room   Mingle loudly.

The Imperial Houses Under Millicent

The 1st Imperial House of Millicent (1975–1976)
H.I.S.M.—Empress I—Millicent
H.I.S.H.—Imperial Crown Princess I—Chatty Cathy Jackson
H.I.S.H.—Imperial Crown Prince I—John

The 2nd Imperial House Under Millicent (1976–1977)
H.I.S.M.—Empress II—Chatty Cathy Jackson
H.I.S.M.—Emperor II—John Reid
H.I.S.H.—Imperial Crown Princess II—Hoopy
H.I.S.H.—Imperial Crown Prince II—Bobby

The 3rd Imperial House Under Millicent (1977–1978)
H.I.S.M.—Empress III—Nikki
H.I.S.M.—Emperor III—Tony
H.I.S.H.—Imperial Crown Princess III—Rayette / Vera
H.I.S.H.—Imperial Crown Prince III—Roy

The 4th Imperial House Under Millicent (1978–1979)
H.I.S.M.—Empress IV—Rayette
H.I.S.M.—Emperor IV—Micheal
H.I.S.H.—Imperial Crown Princess IV—Bubbles
H.I.S.H.—Imperial Crown Prince IV—Ron

The 5th Imperial House of The Undersea World of Atlantis
(1979–1980)
H.I.S.M.—Empress V—Trixie
H.I.S.M.—Emperor V—Joe Boy
H.I.S.H.—Imperial Crown Princess V—Loni
H.I.S.H.—Imperial Crown Prince V—Sam

The 6th Imperial House of Polaris—The Star Court (1981–1982)
H.I.S.M.—Empress VI—Lindee Star
H.I.S.M.—Emperor VI—Daryl
H.I.S.H.—Imperial Crown Princess VI—Mrs. K.
H.I.S.H.—Imperial Crown Prince VI—Sam

The 7th Imperial House of The Mega Mentals (1982–1983)
H.I.S.M.—Empress VII—Mrs. K.
H.I.S.M.—Emperor VII—Sam
H.I.S.H.—Imperial Crown Princess VII—Lexi Con
H.I.S.H.—Imperial Crown Prince VII—Trash

The 8th Imperial House of The Crazy Eights (1983–1984)
H.I.S.M.—Empress VIII—Mary Mess
H.I.S.M.—Emperor VIII—Rick
H.I.S.H.—Imperial Crown Princess VIII—Lexi Con
H.I.S.H.—Imperial Crown Prince VIII—Greg

The 9th Imperial House of Dirty Diamonds (1984–1985)
H.I.S.M.—Empress IX—Lulu LaRude
H.I.S.M.—Emperor IX—Buster Boxx
H.I.S.H.—Imperial Crown Princess IX—Gloria Hole
H.I.S.H.—Imperial Crown Prince IX—Mike

The 10th Imperial House of Divine Excellence & Motherly Love
(1985–1986)
H.I.S.M.—Empress X—Amii L. Nitrate (abdicated)
H.I.S.M.—Empress X—Mother Jean
H.I.S.M.—Emperor X—Mr. X
H.I.S.H.—Imperial Crown Princess X—Tina / Cassandra
H.I.S.H.—Imperial Crown Prince X—Don

The 11th Imperial House of Age & Adventure (1986–1987)
H.I.S.M.—Emperor XI—Sig
H.I.S.M.—Empress XI—Beverly Crest
H.I.S.H.—Imperial Crown Prince XI—Don
H.I.S.H.—Imperial Crown Princess XI—Ora Fice

The 12th Imperial House of Vicious Knights & Imperial Pleasures
(198–1988)
H.I.S.M.—Empress XII—Ora Fice
H.I.S.M.—Emperor XII—Teddy Bear
H.I.S.H.—Imperial Crown Princess XII—Mandy Kamp
H.I.S.H.—Imperial Crown Prince XII—Perry

The 13th Imperial House of Pitbulls & Poodles (1988–1989)
H.I.S.M.—Empress XIII—Gracie
H.I.S.M.—Emperor XIII—Jim
H.I.S.H.—Imperial Crown Princess XIII—Brandi Bodeen
H.I.S.H.—Imperial Crown Prince XIII—Kevin

The 14th Imperial House of Silver Tongs & Dance (1989–1990)
H.I.S.M.—Empress XIV—Leah Way
H.I.S.M.—Emperor XIV—Rob
H.I.S.H.—Imperial Crown Princess XIV—Twiggy
H.I.S.H.—Imperial Crown Prince XIV—Pepe

The Most Excellent 15th Imperial House of Divining Rod . . . A New
Decade (1990–1991)
H.I.S.M.—Empress XV—Twiggy
H.I.S.M.—Emperor XV—Pierre
H.I.S.H.—Imperial Crown Princess XV—Jackie 2 Step
H.I.S.H.—Imperial Crown Prince XV—Nellie Michael

The 16th Imperial House of Women on the Edge (1991–1992)
H.I.S.M.—Empress XVI—Mandy Kamp
H.I.S.M.—Emperor XVI—Brian
H.I.S.H.—Imperial Crown Princess XVI—Ginger Snapped
H.I.S.H.—Imperial Crown Prince XVI—Darryl

The Recycled Environmentally Friendly 17th Imperial House of
Androgyny (1992–1993)
H.I.S.M.—Empress XVII—Mary Mess
H.I.S.M.—Emperor XVII—Mr. Vera
H.I.S.H.—Imperial Crown Princess XVII—Marsha Black ,
H.I.S.H.—Imperial Crown Prince XVII—Toni Curtis

The 18th Imperial Carrot House of Life, Liberty & the Pursuit . . .
(1993–1994)
H.I.S.M.—Empress XVIII—Marsha Black
H.I.S.M.—Emperor XVIII—Toni Curtis
H.I.S.H.—Imperial Crown Princess XVIII—Gretchen Wilder
H.I.S.H.—Imperial Crown Prince XVIII—Jim

The 19th Imperial House of G.I. Gals & Glamorous Joes (1994–1995)
H.I.S.M.—Empress XIX—Gretchen Wilder
H.I.S.M.—Emperor XIX—Jim
H.I.S.H.—Imperial Crown Princess XIX—Natasha
H.I.S.H.—Imperial Crown Prince XIX—Horst

The 20th Imperial Color Coordinated House of Lace, Lamé &
Lounge Acts (1995–1996)
H.I.S.M.—Empress XX—Tootsanelda Whoofenpeekhole
H.I.S.M.—Emperor XX—Mr. Vera
H.I.S.H.—Imperial Crown Princess XX—Weena Luv
H.I.S.H.—Imperial Crown Prince XX—Jim

The 21st Imperial House of Turn-A-Bout is Fair Play (1996–1997)
No Empress XXI
H.I.S.M.—Emperor XXI—Signy Chaise St. Claire
H.I.S.H.—Imperial Crown Princess XXI—Endora
H.I.S.H.—Imperial Crown Prince XXI—Ed

The 22nd Imperial House Under Millicent (1997–1998)
H.I.S.M.—Empress XXII—Jackie Two-Step
H.I.S.M.—Emperor Regent—Brian
H.I.S.H.—Imperial Crown Princess XXII—Roxanne Hurd-Pride
H.I.S.H.—Imperial Crown Prince XXII—Scott

The 23rd Imperial House of Luv (1998–1999)
H.I.S.M.—Empress XXIII—Weena Luv
H.I.S.H.—Imperial Crown Princess XXIII—Ida Claire
H.I.S.H.—Imperial Crown Princess XXIII—Sticky Vicky
H.I.S.H.—Imperial Crown Prince XXIII—Chris D'Party

The 24th Dynasty of Ebony & Ivory with Fried Chicken, Watermelon
and Ta Ta's for Days (1999–2000)
H.I.S.M.—Empress XXIV—Dyna Thirst
H.I.S.M.—Emperor XXIV—Gary
H.I.S.H.—Imperial Crown Princess XXIV—Dezyna Gowan
H.I.S.H.—Imperial Crown Prince XXIV—Gaily Forward

The 25th Imperial House Under Millicent (2000–2001)
H.I.S.M.—Empress XXV—Mr. Vera
H.I.S.M.—Emperor XXV—Ron
H.I.S.H.—Imperial Crown Princess XXV—Ida Claire
H.I.S.H.—Imperial Crown Prince XXV—Jim
H.I.S.H.—Imperial Crown Prince XXV—Rob

The 26th Imperial House of The Fun That Was Lost But Not Forgotten
(2001–2002)
H.I.S.M.—Empress XXVI—Ida Claire WPCC
H.I.S.M.—Emperor XXVI—Rob Bigonion WPCC
H.I.S.H.—Imperial Crown Princess XXVI—Ladonna
H.I.S.H.—Imperial Crown Prince XXVI—Bobby

The 27th Imperial House of Blah Blah Blah & What a Pity
(2002–2003)
H.I.S.M.—Empress XXVII—Endora St. Claire
H.I.S.M.—Emperor XXVII—Bobby Bigonion
H.I.S.H.—Imperial Crown Princess XXVII—Bianca
H.I.S.H.—Imperial Crown Princess XXVII—Krystall Ball
H.I.S.H.—Imperial Crown Prince XXVII—Mark

The 28th Imperial House of Never Ending Sunsets & Everlasting
Fantasies (2003–2004)
H.I.S.M.—Empress XXVIII—Cleo Oprah Patra
H.I.S.M.—Emperor XXVIII—Rob Bigonion WPCC
H.I.S.H.—Imperial Crown Princess XXVIII—Sticky Vicky

The 29th Imperial House Under Millicent (2004–2005)
H.I.S.M.—Empress XXIX—Sticky Vicky
H.I.S.M.—Emperor Co-Regent—Ron
H.I.S.M.—Emperor Co-Regent—Jim
H.I.S.H.—Imperial Crown Princess XXIX—Lloyd Blue-Em-All
H.I.S.H.—Imperial Crown Princess XXIX—Southern Comfort

The 30th Imperial House of XXX-travagent XXX-tasy & XXX-rated Erotica (2005–2006)
H.I.S.M.—Empress XXX—Leah Way
H.I.S.M.—Emperor XXX—Lloyd Blue-Em-All
H.I.S.H.—Imperial Crown Princess XXX—Marni Gras
H.I.S.H.—Imperial Crown Prince XXX—Jamal Patra Blue-Em-All

The 31st Imperial House of Northern Lights and Southern Delights (2006–2007)
H.I.S.M.—Empress XXXI—Southern Comfort
H.I.S.M.—Emperor XXXI—Chuck Lonestar
H.I.S.H.—Princess XXXI—Elise She Showed Up
H.I.S.H.—Prince XXXI—Sundance

THE OFFICIAL CROWNED HEADS OF CLUB FLASHBACK
(or Divas with a bar tab)
1976-1991

Mz. Flashback 1—Millie / Mr. Flashback 1—Joey
Mz. Flashback 2—Felicia / Mr. Flashback 2—Bobby
Mz. Flashback 3—Gino / Mr. Flashback 3—Roy
Mz. Flashback 4—Bianca Bang-Bang / Mr. Flashback 4—Mr. Vera
Mz. Flashback 5—Gracie / Mr. Flashback 5—Leonard
Mz. Flashback 6—Tina / Mr. Flashback 6—Lee
Mz. Flashback 7—Trash / Mr. Flashback 7—David
Mz. Flashback 8—Lexi Con / Mr. Flashback 8—Gerry
Mz. Flashback 9—Gloria Hole / Mr. Flashback 9—Mr. K.247
Mz. Flashback 10—Tallulah / Mr. Flashback 10—Dorky-Louise
Mz. Flashback 11—Twiggy / Mr. Flashback 11—Neon
Mz. Flashback 12—Kim Burly / Mr. Flashback 12—Deejay
Mz. Flashback 13—Cleo / Mr. Flashback 13—Zola
Mz. Flashback 14—Gretchen Wilder / Mr. Flashback 14—Hansel
Mz. Flashback 15—a) Christine, 15—b) Leah Weigh, 15—c) Ginger Snapped, 15—d) Mandy Kamp

THE OFFICIAL APPOINTED ENTERTAINERS OF THE YEAR

I. Chatty Cathy Jackson (1982)
II. Mrs. K. and Sam (1983)
III. Lindee Star (1984)
IV. Lulu LaRude (1985)
V. Gloria Hole (1986)
VI. Twiggy (1987)
VII. Kim Burly (1988)
VIII. Cleo (1989)
IX. Twiggy (1990)
X. Mandy Kamp (1991)
XI. Beverly Crest (1992)
XII. Kristy Krunt (1993)
XIII. Neon (1994)
XIV. The Village People (1995)
XV. Rosa Rita Refried Beans (1996)
XVI. Tootzenelda Woofenpeekhole (1997)

After this, the award shifted from an appointed position to a popular vote and continues to be awarded to this day.

THE OFFICIAL APPOINTED ENTERTAINERS OF THE DECADE

the '70s
Entertainer of the Decade I
Chatty Cathy Jackson

the '80s
Entertainer of the Decade II
Gloria Hole

the '90s
Entertainer of the Decade III
Twiggy

The Gospel According to
The Hole Family

The Big Onion Chapter

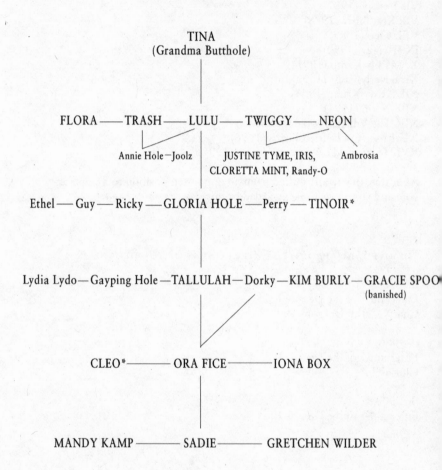

TINA
(Grandma Butthole)

FLORA —— TRASH —— LULU —— TWIGGY —— NEON

Annie Hole–Joolz

JUSTINE TYME, IRIS,
CLORETTA MINT, Randy-O

Ambrosia

Ethel —— Guy —— Ricky —— GLORIA HOLE —— Perry —— TINOIR*

Lydia Lydo–Gayping Hole —TALLULAH— Dorky—KIM BURLY—GRACIE SPOO
(banished)

CLEO* ———— ORA FICE ———— IONA BOX

MANDY KAMP ———— SADIE ———— GRETCHEN WILDER

CAPITALS denotes QUEENS, other names are friends.
* denotes foster children

The Queen Is Born

AT EDMONTON'S LOUD & QUEER CABARET in 1995, I wrote my first story.

It was the Lulu chapter from the beginning of the book. I read it in front of the audience. They laughed. The story wasn't true (Lulu never had a run-in with a serial killer with a foot fetish), but the picture of Lulu that I had drawn with my words resonated somehow.

I didn't know it at the time, but it was the first step on a journey that has lasted over a decade.

I remember CJSR Gaywire host / producer Kristy Harcourt approaching me and saying, "Can you do me favour?"

"Of course," I answered.

"Keep writing," she said.

Emboldened by the response, I wrote a story about Tallulah's epileptic seizure in the drag room. Then a story about Ora's funeral. Then Empress I, Millie, passed away, and I wrote a eulogy for her funeral.

It occurred to me that I could work this material into a one-man play, something I had been wanting to try for some time. I approached Ron Jenkins to direct me, and we created the first draft of *The Edmonton Queen* for the 1996 Edmonton International Fringe Festival, nine years after Guys In Disguise had first emerged into the limelight.

The show was forty-five minutes long. I performed it as myself, not as Gloria. Mandy Kamp did drag to create shadow portraits of the Queens in the story behind a giant screen. Neon was the stage manager.

It was terrifying . . . I knew how to perform, but I learned

Gretchen Wilder as Empress XIX, 1995.

how to act during that run. It was thrilling to see that the stories of my friends mattered, not just to the people who knew them, but to many more.

The day my Mom came to see the show she sat next to publisher Candas Jane Dorsey, who approached me as we cleared the stage after the show.

"Are there more stories you could write about?" she asked.

"Of course," I answered. "So many."

"Then keep writing. There's a book in here."

I went to Halifax to visit Lulu and give her a copy of the script. The next time I saw her, in Calgary, I gave her the huge pile of pages that would become the book. It was Mother's Day.

The summer of '97, I received the Sterling Award for Outstanding New Fringe Work.

A few weeks later, I held the book in my hands. I pulled two copies out of the box and signed one to Lulu, and one to myself. I sent hers to Halifax. Lulu didn't have the proper ID to pick it up, so for a week, she harassed and threatened the people at the shipping company until they just gave it her.

I got the chance to tour the country with the book as my calling card. Each launch was unique, from the drag show in Halifax, to the sit-down dinner and Value Village fashion show that accompanied my reading in Saskatoon. In Vancouver, Little Sisters packed Doll & Penny for a night. In Edmonton, we hung gowns by Tootsenelda Woofenpeekhole all around the Rice Theatre lobby.

A few years went by, and I got the chance to perform the play again. But the original play was already obsolete. The old play wasn't good enough, and the book was too long. Distilling parts of the book into shorter form didn't make a good play either, so I went back to the drawing board and started writing again.

New Year's Eve 2000, the last First Night Festival, was the launch of the new and improved EQ. Almost half of it was new material. At the first performance, a bunch of men left as I got to the final chapter: the "eulogy." I guess by that time they had figured out I wasn't going to do a Marilyn impersonation and decided to cut their losses. The second performance went much better, and the audience leapt to its feet at the end.

I performed the new version at the Edmonton International Street Performer's Festival. The throne on stage was surrounded by thousands of photos—snapshots of the years Lulu and I terrorized The Big Onion, and the cast of thousands that experienced it with us.

At Winnipeg's annual Fringe, I did the show in a now-infamous venue that had been an arson hit a month earlier. I sat in the back, smelling the stale smoke and trying not to touch anything before I went on stage.

We did one last run of the play in Edmonton at the 2001 Fringe. The first couple of nights I was worried that I had trotted this pony out one-too-many times. But then the reviews hit and the rest of the run sold out.

October, 2001, at Regina's Globe Theatre, the show was coupled with the Loud & Queer Festival, and there were protesters outside with signs saying "Sodomy kills more Canadians a year than handguns." There was a picture of a gun with a green circle around it (good), and a bad drawing of two men holding hands, with the red line through it (bad).

During the Regina run, I called Jenkins in Edmonton to talk about the show.

"How's it going?" he asked.

"I don't know . . . I think this is the last time I do this show."

"Really? Why?"

"I'm just not feeling it, Ron. It's not affecting me the way it used to."

We talked about how it might be time to move on. Maybe the grieving was finally over.

That night, the Girls showed me they weren't done with me yet. Somehow, the play broke my heart all over again.

But, as it turns out, it was the last time I performed the play. I started talking about it, and the book, in the past tense.

When Ruth Linka (Brindle & Glass) approached me in 2006 about an anniversary edition of *The Edmonton Queen*, it sounded deceptively simple. I didn't realize that revisiting your work a decade later is a frightening proposition.

A decade ago, I was a drag queen writing a fairy tale. Now, I am a writer looking back at a first step in a career. I can see where it flies, and where it fails. There are parts that make me cringe, and parts that make me laugh. Here and there, I have included excerpts from the play. For the most part, I have left the stories intact. The fairy tale is what it is. It's the story I needed to tell at that time.

But I have learned to never refer to *The Edmonton Queen* in the past tense, because I will probably keep coming back to it in one form or another, until the day I stop writing. To date, I have written three plays and several short stories, and book-and-a-half, and more essays than I can count about the Flashback years.

And I haven't even started yet.

John Reid.

Flashback

First published in SEE Magazine *in the*
Pride Issue, June 16, 2005.

FIRST OF ALL, IT WAS CALLED FLASHBACK, not Flashbacks.
Unlike the other nightclubs of its time, it felt no compulsion
to pluralize. If you were hip enough, you called it Flash. But
if you were really in the know, it was just The Club. That's all
you had to say to let people know where to meet you, because
to its punked-out drag-queen-freaky denizens (and all their
fans), there simply was no other place to spend your weekend
in Edmonton.

If you were a visiting celebrity and asked your roadie/
concierge/drug dealer to find out where the cool people partied
in Edmonton, you would be told to head to Flashback. If you
were anything outside of purely hetero, Flashback was the one
place in town to explore the possibilities. If you were a rich
young Oiler looking for a place to be simultaneously fawned
over and ignored, you would grab your buddies and head to
Flashback.

But most of all, if you were a radical, a visionary, a fashion
statement, or an outcast, you would eventually find yourself in
the block-long line that stretched as far as The Foxy Lady Disco
Dancing Lounge, waiting patiently to be allowed in to frolic
with the freaks. Or as Joni Mitchell once said:

Fuck it! Tonight I'm going dancing
With the drag queens and the punks.
Big beat deliver me from this sanctimonious skunk.

She could have been talking about the way one could
completely disappear in Flashback.

And disappear they did. Over the sixteen years of its existence, how many thousands? No one can say. Much like Woodstock, if everyone who says "I used to go to Flashback" had actually gone, The Club would have hosted hundreds of thousands.

And maybe it did. For many, Flashback was the first taste of the underworld. For others, it was the birthplace of a future.

Most importantly, it was a confirmation that the world didn't have to be the way it was. Flashback was the proof. Within those walls, a new order was being established.

Flashback had three distinct manifestations. The first Club was in a basement on Jasper Avenue, currently known as Marg's Upholstery. Cramped, hot, sweaty, and impossible to get into, it quickly became the magnet for the Big Onion's non-boring elite. It was literally bursting at the seams when it moved to its most revered location on 104th Street. In this location, the reputation of Flashback quickly led to international acclaim. Now it has been transformed into luxury condos; I always wonder who's living on the dance floor, who's having sex in the sound booth. Thoughts like these bring me much comfort.

The third Flashback, a short-lived white elephant in a cold cavern under the 5th Street Bridge, was a sad final chapter—the whimper at the end of a scream. The final night saw the staff removing tons of sound and lighting equipment after the last last call, in what must have been one of the wildest midnight moves in history.

The concept for Flashback was born when a young John Reid, having finally mustered up the guts to come out of the closet and go to Club 70 (now Boots & Saddle), was barred entry at the door because the homo letting people in thought he looked too straight. Reid, shattered by the exclusion, had to be signed in by a member willing to vouch for him. Club 70 had a gay-exclusive policy, meaning the straight friends of its gay members weren't allowed entry. Even Mother Jean (Imperial Gay Mother of All Alberta, and best friend and roommate to many of Edmonton's early gender-benders) wasn't welcome.

Once inside, Reid saw lesbians fighting and gay men standing around looking fabulous. But Club 70 didn't have a DJ . . . only a jukebox. The problem with this, according to Reid, was that the lesbians always arrived at the bar first and plugged the jukebox full of requests for polkas and country music.

Reid applied to be on the board of directors of Club 70. He also started travelling, visiting queer clubs in the US, where he saw what made them work: "It was always the music," he remembers. His main mission became to get Club 70 to invest in a sound system and a DJ. After a few years of this, Reid, along with several other collaborators, including the future Empress I of Edmonton, Millie (who knew *everything* about Donna Summer, and who also later became the very first Mz. Flashback), started Flashback in its 116th Street location with a very specific mandate: to prevent reverse discrimination and provide a venue for gay people and *all* of their friends.

When Flash became the place to be in the Big Onion, the Club moved to the larger 104th Street location, but none of Reid's early partners stayed in the business.

I first stepped into Flash in 1982. It already had seven or eight years of life, liberty, and the pursuit of glamour-addiction under its leopard-skin belt. There were already Legends who had been created and destroyed, icons who had moved on, a past that screamed its secrets. I heard about them all. Flashback had an oral tradition other than the one I kept seeing drag queens practicing on drunk straight boys in the pot-smoke-filled, mixed-gender, toilet-water-flooded bathrooms.

Part of Flashback's history is the public battles it fought over the years. Flashback was a private club. In the era of its birth, this was essential. Gay clubs were new in Edmonton. It was felt that an exclusive membership list would weed out troublemakers like homophobes and murderers. But the private club status that limited access also became a feature the Alberta Liquor Control Board loved using to exclude the gay bars from the relaxation of the liquor laws. Yes, my darlings, a time existed when one's drinking had to stop at 1:00 AM.

So the private clubs (gay bars) in Alberta lobbied the ALCB (straight white guys with patronage positions) to relax the liquor laws and extend the drinking hours. After much thought, the ALCB agreed, and changed the rules . . . for *all* bars in Alberta *except* private clubs. Suddenly everyone was drinking until 2 AM except those queer freaks (private clubs like the policemen's club, with 24-hour liquor service, remained unaffected by the change). So Flashback led the charge to level the playing field. It won, eventually, and the counterculture got to stay up as late as the rest of the province.

That, however, was just part of the battle. The ALCB was constantly sneaking undercover into the Club to catch us in any number of violations, from the bathrooms falling apart to having too many people in the Club. Every time this happened, we cheerfully took the weekend off, had the "SUSPENDED" sign framed in gold, painted something black, and opened the next weekend "NEWLY RENOVATED."

The long battle Flashback had with the ALCB went on for a decade; when the liquor officials passed a ruling, the proprietor had no recourse but to appeal the decision, whereupon the case would go before the ALCB's own kangaroo court. This appeal board would often overturn the ruling of its own officials and pass the recommendation back, only to have it completely ignored by the ALCB, which was under absolutely no compulsion to accept the decisions of its appeal board. After several cases where this occurred, Flashback took the ALCB to court. This had never happened before, and was a win in itself. The result was that bar owners finally had a way to challenge discriminatory practices by the ALCB and its inspectors. Shortly after, the Alberta Liquor Act was rewritten, effectively crushing the long hierarchy of the ALCB. It was disbanded and replaced with the Alberta Gaming and Liquor Commission.

As visible as Flashback was the list of Queens known as Mz. Flashback. When the *Edmonton Sun*'s page eight written by Wayne Crouse was in its infancy, Mz. Flashback 7, Trash, was regularly featured in its gossip file. Trash was different than his foresisters, for he adored donning a wig and dress and heading to public events like Date Night at K-Days, and sometimes joining parades as they marched by. In the pre-Famous-Drag-Queen days, Trash was ballsy, unafraid, and highly visible. So when Trash resigned in a huff over not being cast as Marilyn Monroe in the annual Halloween Show, the media wrote about it. In fact, the whole queer town talked of nothing else that month.

The Flashback drag mascots were like glamorous centrepieces for a burgeoning visibility. One year the annual Mr. and Mz. Flashback party, all in drag and on their way to the pageant in limousines, got caught in an Oilers mob, celebrating a Stanley Cup win. Eight drag queens and their escorts had to exit said limousine in the middle of the riot and make a beeline for the Club a few blocks away.

Flashback hosted some pretty high-end events in its time. In addition to the annual Mz. Flashback Pageant and the infamous Halloween show, there were happenings like the International Designer of the Year Award. I remember the pep talk we queer waiters received, instructing us on how to hobnob with the rich and powerful. One of those rich and powerfuls was the wife of then-Premier Peter Lougheed. When she tried to check her fur coat, she was told by the coat check girl that there was not enough room. When the always polite Jeannie Lougheed urged "Surely you have room for the Premier's wife's coat," she was told "I don't care of you're the Queen of fucking England, the coat check is full!" Exit coat check girl, enter local media, all clamouring to find out why Alberta's First Lady was hanging out at a gay bar. The Flashback dance floor was also featured on local TV when ITV rented the Club to shoot a weekly aerobics workout show.

The private club status worked against Flashback at times: the Club wasn't allowed to advertise anywhere. So when Canadian drag icon Craig Russell came to town to launch his comeback (the one that ended his career), word had to be spread in creative ways. Enter Donna Marie Artuso, who as the new page eight writer kept the Flash gossip front and centre for those who cared. She was also the annual celebrity judge for the Mz. Gay Cup Pageant for a few years. (She stopped accepting our invitation when a severed head won the pageant. She felt that was in bad taste, even for us. For the record, the severed head performed "These Boots Are Made For Walking" for the talent portion of the pageant.)

The community Flashback served was in its infancy; as the Club matured, so did its denizens and their politics. Always front and centre within the brick walls of Flashback, gay rights took forever to catch on in Alberta. In addition to early Pride Events, Flashback hosted fashion, art, and theatre fundraisers constantly. Through these events people were exposed to the Club and the amazing four-storey brick building it resided in. Artists and musicians began setting up shop in the offices and lofts: Rod Wolfe launched some of his many musical ventures from his rented warehouse space on the second floor; metal sculptors Isla Burns and Clay Ellis set up a shared space in the basement; photographers Richard Seimans and Brenda Bastell both launched their careers in the offices upstairs.

As well, the legions of early Queens began growing up and starting careers and businesses, putting their people skills to work in other ways. Lulu and Gloria began getting professional drag bookings at straight events, Trash became an artist who worked with garbage, Lindee Star established Swizzlesticks, a successful salon in Edmonton, Cleo left for Vancouver to become an actor, and Guys in Disguise went on to perform at their first Fringe. The Flashback network expanded faster than the Tory surplus during a desert war. The Flash queens began appearing more often in the media, being the camera magnets that they were. Many moved to other cities, and ran for pageants, and became Empresses elsewhere.

By the late '80s, Flashback had a reputation that had spread far past Alberta. *Graffiti Magazine* put Flashback on its list of the top five clubs in North America, calling it "Edmonton's Alternative Underground" (within a month, The Roost scooped the slogan, giving its upstairs room the same name). A New

York DJ wrote in *Billboard* that Flashback was one of the two best clubs in Canada. Brad Fraser set many scenes in his play *Unidentified Human Remains and the True Nature of Love* in Flashback. When I saw the play on opening night in an off-off-Broadway theatre, it thrilled me that now New York would hear about the place I loved so much. The Denys Arcand film version spread the word even wider. Celebrities and commoners alike who hung out at Flashback and then moved away took with them tales of amazing music, a dance floor that throbbed for eight hours straight every Saturday night, the two hour drag shows, the insane bathrooms, the hot men, the hot chicks, that guy that danced with the scarf, and if they were lucky, the sound booth with its tens of thousands of records, special after-hours cocktails, the drag pit, the kitchen parties, drag queens in the beer fridge cooling their feet off, the dog that jumped off the roof, the party on the loading dock, the drugs, the way the bartenders bitched you out in front of everyone when you didn't tip, the blow job in the downstairs bathroom, and the stumbling into the sunlight at 6 AM wondering what the fuck just happened.

Nowadays, not a month goes by when I don't receive an email from someone I haven't seen in decades, or when I don't run into someone saying, "I miss Flashback. Why can't there be a place like that now?"

"It could never happen again," predicts Reid, "not in the same way. Flashback's success wasn't just the music and the building, or even the party. It was the people who came, in droves, that made it what it was. Those people were a product of the time we lived in. Those people needed a place where gay, straight, and all shades of grey in between could coexist. They were all attracted to Flash for the same reason: it matched their philosophy, and it showed them that philosophy at work. And it was a beautiful thing to see."

And now many more may have a chance to see it. Patrick Monaghan was technical director at Flashback from 1980 to 1983, when the Club began producing drag shows that rivalled all others. He has guarded some of the original tapes of those performances and is now in the process of digitally rescuing/preserving them for generations to come. A few weeks ago, I received the DVD of the first drag show I ever saw in person. I get the same chills watching the show now as I did on Halloween in 1982—except this time I'm not on acid. On this DVD I can see all of the performers, none of whom I knew then, many of whom would end up being my dearest friends. And they're young and beautiful and full of life. That drag show changed my life forever. Two and a half months later, my alter ego Gloria stepped onto that stage for the first time.

For Monaghan, who worked in Edmonton's TV industry in the early '80s, those years mark a time when he got the chance to contribute creatively to the burgeoning queer community. He has "profoundly affectionate memories of that time."

"I've babied these tapes since I left Edmonton years ago," he laughs. The newly restored drag shows look even better than the original footage. "As people began to pass, it seemed more and more important to preserve this, and to share it. For those in the videos, and for those who knew the people in them, it's a record of a seminal time in their lives," he explains. "People came out because of Flash. It changed all of our lives."

Preserving the Flashback tapes is a small first step in archiving the copious amount of Flashback evidence: the hundreds of videotapes, the thousands of photos, the millions of friends and memories. Monaghan wants to begin the huge process of connecting all those dots. If you can help, he can be reached at flashbackproject@shaw.ca. If you were ever in one of those shows, or had a friend or family member who was, contact can be made. Monaghan hopes that a grassroots movements like this will help archive the early years of the Canadian gay community's emergence: "Those of us who are left behind have an obligation and a responsibility."

Reid seems, like many of us, hard-pressed to find the words to describe the feelings of that era. "It's always there, in the back of my mind . . . and I always miss it," Reid says. "I miss the fun, the camaraderie, the silliness . . . all the people, all the friends. I don't miss the war with the ALCB or the broken-down toilets that always flooded during last call. But I was proud to be fighting on the right side. I always felt as though I had as much support from the straight community as I did from the gay community. I was shell-shocked when it ended, though, and I entered the whole Rebar experience very reluctantly." It was the Flashback sound and lighting equipment that was used to start Rebar, with for many years was the hottest nightclub on Whyte Avenue.

When Rebar ended, Reid hung up the dance club shoes for good. "On the bright side, life has some normalcy now. And I use my experiences a lot." Reid now teaches kids on reserves, "kids with issues. I learned from those years how to crisis-manage, how to think quick on my feet. And whether it's issues of sexuality, or substance abuse, none of it fazes me. Because of Flashback, I've seen it all before."

Darrin Hagen in Michel Tremblay's "Hosanna."

The Bigger Picture

These are my snapshots. Now, if this were my mother's photo album, everything would be blown up to portrait size, mounted under sticky Cellophane in chronological order, with little ballpoint labels telling you who's who.

But this is my family album. They're just snapshots, because at the time I didn't think a full portrait was necessary. They're just snapshots, a little out of focus because it was all moving pretty fast. They're just snapshots, but there are thousands of them . . . overflowing, spilling out of boxes and basements . . . shining, perfect moments frozen forever like the river in winter.

—from The Edmonton Queen, *the play*

When writing *The Edmonton Queen*, I did my best to create an insular, self-contained world. But now I see those snapshots were part of a bigger picture: a portrait of gay men who imagined a new order, one where being feminine was neither a drawback nor a curse.

The simple act of identifying the Self. That's all it was. That's how it started.

The ripples moved out from there.

In 1970, *La Duchesse de Langeais* stepped onto the Montreal stage in a whiskey haze. Michel Tremblay's stunning portrait of an aging cross-dressed monarch was heartbreaking and, even now, unique. Her monologue marked the first time the voice of a Queen was heard on a Canadian stage.

She was preceded south of the border, and by only a few years, by Lanford Wilson's Lady Bright in New York. In *The Madness of Lady Bright*, an aging Queen laments the lost loves of her youth in a sweltering New York apartment. It is often referred to as the birth of Queer theatre in North America.

In between those two declarations of identity, there's 1969's Stonewall. And, within weeks, Trudeau's "bedrooms of the nation" speech and the decriminalization of homosexuality. Before that, an almost forgotten act of Queenly defiance called the Compton Café Riot in San Francisco in 1966.

The drag world of North America reared its glamorous head, and it was impossible not to take notice. Tiny acts of defiance, of proclamation.

And yet, when I Google "Canada Drag History," I get race car websites.

It's a bizarre knife-edge that drag performers in Canada balance on. They are alternately worshipped and despised. But drag and its practitioners are, in fact, the politicians and den mothers for emerging queer culture in every city in which they exist. They are the ones who get gossiped about, who spread the gossip, who create the gossip. They are the ones for whom going public is just part of the job, part of the craft they practice.

The Flashback years in Edmonton were creative anarchy, the momentous breaking through of a population demanding to be seen *and* heard. I feel lucky to have been present in the time when drag stood up and insisted on being counted.

Craig Russell shot to international stardom with the debut of *Outrageous* in 1977. I watched him that year (I was in grade seven) on the Genies. It seemed as impossible as it was unlikely that a drag artist would be on national television, presented in a flattering light, entertaining the elite of Canada's showbiz scene. Even more unlikely was that a teenager in a trailer court would watch that performance and follow a similar path. Three decades later, I am so glad I got to see him perform at his height, even if it was just on TV. I didn't realize I was watching history in the making.

On Halloween in 1982, I saw my first Flashback drag show in person. I didn't know anyone on that stage that night, but I had a feeling I was looking at my life. Twenty years later when I watched the newly restored DVD version of that show I knew every person on the stage; some had become my closest friends. Some were instrumental in my early drag career. Some of them I had watched die. I wept as I watched my life unfold.

In 1983, a friend took me to see Tremblay's *Hosanna*. I had just started hanging out with Queens and had done my first few shows. In 1993, I saw *Hosanna* again. My career as a club queen was, for the most part, behind me. I was trying to launch a theatre career. In 2003, I starred as Hosanna alongside Jeff Page's Cuirette at Theatre Network. On closing night, I had trouble controlling the tears all the way through Act Two. Tremblay had written about my life before it happened. And I didn't want it to end. Even the painful stuff. It hurt too beautifully.

FOR SUCH a large country, Canada is just a small town if you're a Queen. The lives and histories swirl and circle around each other.

In 1988, Craig Russell came to Flashback as part of his cross-country comeback tour. The movie was *Too Outrageous*, the follow-up and sequel to the Canadian cult hit *Outrageous* that had made him an international star.

It had been a difficult decade for Craig. The world had changed between the two movies. His tour, promoting the movie and a new disco single called "Glamour Monster," was designed to put him back in the spotlight under which I had first seen him shine. The Master Female Impersonator was an inspiration to all of us in the early '80s. Like us, she had started in the clubs. Like us, she had Delusions of Grandeur.

But by 1988, getting famous by cross-dressing was no longer the exclusive domain of Craig Russell. Boy George and Divine had both stepped into the androgyny of the '80s with hip, wild, confusing styles that didn't rely on looking like a woman . . . and, bolstered by songs that not only packed the dance floor but topped the charts, and by videos that put their amazing genderfuck drag out there for the world to marvel at, they had both become international stars. The timing probably seemed perfect to Russell, even though by the '80s his style of drag was already considered old school.

He arrived in the afternoon. Colin MacLean interviewed Her Majesty for the evening news. Russell had a much-deserved reputation as the reigning Godmother of all of us. He had, after all, reached the top. The whole town was buzzing about the show that night. We felt privileged to meet Russell, and fawned over him appropriately.

I was the pushiest Queen at Flashback, so needless to say I was the mistress of ceremonies for the evening. I was also bartending in Ora's fabulous black and gold beaded dress. My hair was pumped into a massive '80s rat's nest . . . very Dead Or Alive. Many of us girls did glamour drag that night in honour of the Royal Visit. Liz Nicholls and Alan Kellogg were standing at my bar. I had no idea who they were until my charming other half, Kevin, always the publicist, told me to ply them with red wine and butter them up.

Then I closed my bar and went backstage to see if Craig was ready for his show. The Club was packed on a Monday night, an almost impossible feat in those days. I carefully made my way down the stairs, and through the long narrow hallway that led to the drag room.

He sat quietly in front of the mirror, gazing at himself. He wasn't wearing a wig . . . just his own hair bouffed up a bit like he used to do for his Judy Garland character. He was wearing makeup, but not drag makeup. His face didn't really look that different than it had that afternoon: some blush, some eyeliner . . . he might have added lashes to the look, but I couldn't be sure. He was wearing a black poncho with black feathers on it. As Lulu pointed out later, he had one glamour-length nail. Just one.

"Are you ready, Craig?" I asked.

"As ready as I can be," he sighed.

"It's packed out there. They can't wait to see you."

He looked at me in the mirror. His face was tired and sad, but he managed a smile.

"Well, then . . . let's give them what they came for, shall we?"

I walked onstage, grabbed the mike and started my usual

yelling at the audience. They were totally pumped for this auspicious occasion. I introduced Her Highness. They screamed. The music started: Russell's new single, "Glamour Monster." The spotlight hit her.

And the show . . . well, we were all confused. We all kept waiting for the costume changes, for the wigs, for Russell's ladies. He had become famous for his repertoire of impersonations: acts which had set the bar for every drag act that followed in his footsteps. And they never happened. She seemed lost onstage, her voice at times barely rising above the music. The impersonations were, for the most part, barely recognizable.

At the intermission, she headed back to the drag room. Rather than rest, she spent the entire break in the costume pit being interviewed again by Colin MacLean. Thank god we had cleaned it. The Club just kept getting more and more packed with fans. The folks who had seen Act One were positive that the second half of the show would be Pure Russell, the queen that they had come to see.

I walked onstage to do the intro again. The crowd screamed, almost out of control, convinced Russell was saving the best for last. I introduced her. They cheered. I walked backstage to hand her the mike.

"Pop a tuck, darling," I said.

"Wow . . . they love you."

"Darling . . . they can see me any time. They're here to see you."

"Yes . . . but they LOVE you."

She looked me straight in the eye, grabbed the mike out of my hand and said, "Let's do this."

Music . . . smoke machine . . . spotlight . . . and Russell hit the stage and did *the exact same show again.*

Needless to say, the crowd was disappointed. They were polite, but when they saw her in the same outfit as the first act, they gave up hoping for the act they had come to see. Lulu observed: "It looks like she's wearing a feathered Volkswagen seat cover."

Russell's comeback tour got him as far as Toronto. The

"Glamour Monster" single flopped. The movie sequel was universally panned. He ended where he had started twenty years earlier . . . performing in the drag bars he had left to become an international star.

By that time, Lulu had moved to Toronto. She saw La Russell perform one of his final shows at Bar One. By then, Craig was a troubled, dying Queen. Russell stumbled onto the stage, barely lucid and out of his mind on some sort of downer. By the end of the first song, he was unable to stand, and he ended up sitting on the stage, singing incoherently into one of his shoes. The staff came onto the stage and carried him off.

WHEN LULU left Edmonton in the late '80s, it took him a few months to call. Obviously, Rusty Ryan and his troupe "The Great Imposters" had kept him busy all those months.

I met Rusty Ryan when Lulu and I were nineteen. "The Great Imposters" were playing at the Wintergarden Room in Edmonton. The cast at that moment (it was a revolving-door cast of the drag elite of Toronto) was Rusty, Danny Love, and Jackie Loren. The show was fabulous, but even then, in my arrogance and youth, I was sure I could do what they were doing. Lulu and I hung out afterwards. Danny Love and Jackie Loren were sweet as we gushed about the show, their dresses, their numbers, but Rusty invited us up to her room to smoke a joint. There, she gave us the goods: she told us how to do it. How to go pro. She didn't need to see us perform; the mere fact that we wanted it was enough for her. She showed us outfits which, onstage, had looked like a million bucks. Up close, they were cheap skirts with mirror tiles hot-glued in a pattern. "Looks like a million bucks, eh?" she asked, reading our minds and puffing on the joint.

Unlike almost every other queen I had ever met, Rusty felt no need to compete. He was the real thing, and had been doing it for years. A giant of a Queen, he had appeared in both *Outrageous* and its sequel. He was in a Platinum Blonde music video. Never threatened by young, pretty, ambitious queens, he hired those queens and kept them under his wing. But make no mistake: for decades, he was the Boss, and the queens did whatever Rusty told them to do.

The next weekend, we arranged to have "The Great Imposters" come and perform at Flashback. We alternated between the Imposters and our own "Flashback Follies." The crowd cheered and screamed for their hometown girls, and the Imposters gave us a serious run for our money.

Lulu did black drag, and then asked to borrow Danny Love's white feather coat. Needless to say, it got completely ruined over the course of the evening (shades of Tallulah's Grace Jones experience).

I did glamour / rock drag. I remember exactly what I wore that night, because I felt fabulous and got many many many compliments. Was it just the bottom lashes (the one and only time I've ever worn them)? Was it the sassy zebra-print Prince jacket?

Whatever the reason, we held our own that night, surprising everyone.

"The Great Imposters" had one more show in Edmonton that weekend. I didn't go, but Lulu did. When she came back to the Club, she said, "Gloria, I just saw Danny Love do a number that you HAVE to do!" She then described the Life Brand cereal performance. That drag number changed my life. It's still my favourite five minutes onstage.

Rusty's troupe was probably the longest running drag troupe in Canadian history. What made it different (and a unique experience for everyone who worked with him) was that Rusty not only did his shows in gay fars in Toronto, but also produced drag shows in Northern Ontario. His tours hit bars and conventions of straight people in the deep Canadian bush.

MY ONE experience with Jackie Loren happened in Toronto. Lulu had talked the owners of the bar she was working at into flying me and Calgary's darling Justyne Tyme to Hogtown to perform for Gay Pride Week.

In the days after the parade, Jackie was doing Cher

somewhere. I didn't run into her until we were at the after-hours place later (booze can). The booze can had only one bathroom, with no lock. At one point Jackie had to piss. But, she was dressed as Cher. The dragon lady nails never make the urination experience any easier. Part of her under-strapping/padding was a pair of nylons tied around her waist. She was using them as some form of attaching something or holding it in place. It was complicated—I don't really remember how it worked. But I do know that pantyhose can tighten into the tightest knot in history. Jackie tried (in those nails) to undo the knot so she could pee, but to no avail.

"Gloria, help me!" she screamed out the bathroom door. A Sister needed my help. I rushed past the lineup. "Just stand against the door so no one barges in . . . this is gonna be harder than I thought." I leaned my full weight against the door while she struggled to untie the knot in her makeshift attachment device. But by now she had to pee really bad. She did the hop-hop-trying-not-to-pee dance. "I can't do it," she finally admitted. "Help me!"

"Hang on, girl." I pulled her over and tried to undo the knot. But my fingers are huge. There was no way. Her nails were too long. Mine were too short. "Christ, girl, we have to cut it off."

"No! We can't!" she cried. "My outfit will fall apart!"

Someone started banging on the door. Hop-hop-hop-trying-not-to-pee. "Hurry!" she cried.

"Girl, this is not gonna work. Here." I dropped to my knees and started working on the knot with my teeth. The knot started to loosen.

And then the door burst open. And the whole room saw me kneeling in front of Cher, with her pantyhose between my teeth.

CHRISTOPHER PETERSON performs his one man/many women show all over the US.

When Peterson first performed in Edmonton, it was at Lulu's ball. Christopher was the reigning Empress of Vancouver in 1994. Then he spent years in Toronto, honing his impressions, sometimes working with Rusty Ryan. Years later, I worked with Christopher again and again: first in many workshops of the stage version of *Outrageous*, where he displayed his new vocal prowess (doing literally dozens of impersonations live), and then as an anchor member of four Guys In Disguise productions at the Edmonton Fringe.

One day I got a call from a casting agent. This was rare, as I never auditioned for anything and so I was kind of out of the drag casting loop. Plus, most of the drag casting in Canada happened in Vancouver and Toronto, never Alberta. Anyway, the agent was excited about offering me a chance to do a film in drag.

"You'll be a Lucille Ball impersonator."

"But I don't do impersonations," I replied.

"But you do drag . . . couldn't you do Lucy?"

"Not likely. I don't do impersonations. I don't have the wig, the outfit, or the voice."

"Darrin, this could be a very decent opportunity."

I thought back to all the decent drag opportunities I had been eager to grab. Being in drag on location sucked. It was never worth the paltry money (if any) I got from independent films. I always looked awful . . . my drag was something that didn't seem to translate that well to film.

"Then call Christopher Peterson." I gave them his contact number and hung up, smiling as I thought of Christopher tuning the agent in about the reality of what drag costs and how much they would have to pay him.

A year later, I saw a billboard for a new movie: *Rat Race*. The billboard had Cuba Gooding Jr. driving a bus. Over his shoulder was a Lucille Ball impersonator: my sister, Christopher.

Bitch.

TEN YEARS ago, when I launched the first edition of this book in Halifax, I did drag with Lulu. It was the first time I had done drag to launch the book; usually I made other Queens show up in crowns and gowns so I could be the writer. But Lulu and I hadn't done drag together since Flashback, and so we painted our faces at her place and headed off to Reflections for the launch.

Of course, the place was empty, as drag audiences know better than to show up on time. This, of course, made me nervous and I had a drink. Or four. Scotch disappears fast when it passes painted lips. Hours later, we finally had a sizable audience. And for the first time, I had to read from my book while drunk.

Luckily, I could do big parts of it blindfolded. For some reason, I decided to read the closing chapter of the book aloud to close the show.

When I heard sniffling coming from the audience, it took me a moment to realize that it was Lulu crying. It's one thing to read those words, and quite another to hear them out loud. The list of names—just names, that's all they are—is still enough to break my heart. Those names represent so much to anyone who knew them. Group those names together, and they become not only a cast of brilliant characters, but a lifetime of inspiration and sadness, a way of life, a version of the world that relies on courage and sheer will.

The evening ended, as did so many of the evenings Lulu and I shared, with me passed out on her kitchen floor. Of course, there's a picture of it. Lulu's kitten, Oswald, looks at me with concern.

I MET Quentin Crisp briefly, in 1991. I was much shyer back then. I kick myself for not knowing more, for not realizing how important he was to my world. If I could meet him now . . . I was in New York seeing *Unidentified Human Remains and the True Nature of Love* open off-off-Broadway. My travel buddy Andy and I gazed at the famous skyline as we came in for a landing. Andy quipped, "Hey, we should call up Quentin Crisp and take him out for breakfast." I scoffed at the idea, sure that La Crisp had better queens than us to lunch with.

Opening night, and there he is. I recognize him from the *Blueboy* magazines I used to shoplift when I was a kid. He looks, as always, like a Grand Old Dame, hat perched just so, that look of mild feminine annoyance/surprise on his face. I greet him briefly, and choose not to gush, as most are doing, but instead just give him a Queenly nod of recognition.

Years later, when Crisp passes, I start pouring through the things he wrote, the things written about him, and I realize that Andy was right. Crisp was famous for meeting anybody who ever called him. As long as you bought him breakfast, he would go into performance mode for as long as you looked interested . . . or until you paid the bill. No audience was too small.

During World War II, Quentin Crisp was denied entry into the British Army by the medical board on the grounds that he was "suffering from sexual perversion" because he refused to deny his effeminate destiny. His response was to stock up on henna and cosmetics and draw as much attention as possible to his lack of masculine attributes, parading through the London Blitz of 1941 with bright red hair and a nearly full face of makeup.

I guess that would make Crisp Queen Mother Ultima.

I HATE movies about drag. Seeing films like *To Wong Fu* just makes me cranky. I never enjoy seeing some straight actor "proving" he's straight in the press interviews. I hate seeing the flaws in the portrayals. Even worse, I hate seeing it when the filmmakers get it right and show our world the way it is; then, it can make me cringe.

There are exceptions: *Priscilla, Queen of the Desert* is probably every Queen's favourite drag homage. And the documentary about the Compton's Café riot made me proud to be a gender outlaw of sorts. But generally, when I see a Hollywood version of our lives on the screen, I see exactly what Hollywood does best: trivialize and oversimplify.

But I saw a documentary once, shot in the early '60s in black and white, of the Crowning of a Queen. I don't know the title because I missed the beginning, and haven't yet found anything about it, but I'll never forget it. The exciting thing about it was that there was no commentary, no "writing," no editorializing. They just pointed the camera at the action and watched it unfold. It's in some large hall in New York. You see the backstage prep. You see them arrive. You see the pageant. The Queens fight for that crown. One of them storms off the stage in protest when the winner is announced (a young, thin, pretty, inexperienced Queen). After the show, there's a showdown in the lobby between the winner and the angry loser and all her supporters. Insults fly. The police are called. The cameras keep running. The last image, after the cops break up the near riot, is of the young winner. It's later that evening, and he's out of drag now. He looks like a young femmy David Bowie. He's sitting in a phone booth in what must be Grand Central Station, with his new crown in his hands. He just sits there and looks at it. The camera pans back, gradually revealing the daily pedestrian traffic that flows non-stop like blood through the veins of the city. A Queen is born . . . and the world just keeps passing by, unaware of the presence of Royalty.

TO BE a Queen in Canada, one needs a bigger set of balls than most men will ever have. In thousands of shows, for hundreds of fans at a time, every one of these men put it all out there. The world of drag has existed in a public sphere for four decades now in Canada and the US. And every single act of defiance rests on the shoulders of the act before it. From Christine Jorgensen's infamous gender transformation in 1950, to the Queens in the Regina Gay Pride Parade last summer, there have always been men willing to cross that line that was drawn in the sandbox in front of them at the age of two.

These Queens live lives of magic and courage. Whether they continue to perform in the bars, or venture into the light of day, they stand up to the world. Even though it seems completely blasé now, it was audacious, and even a dangerous life, twenty years ago.

The simple act of identifying the Self. That's all it is. That's how it starts. The ripples move out from there.

They are my sisters, friends, and for a dizzying quarter-century, they were my collaborators and heroes.

Their dignity is also mine.

Final Voyage

I GOT OFF THE AIRPLANE IN HALIFAX expecting to see security everywhere. It was September 11, five years after *the* September 11, and I knew from watching the news that Condoleeza Rice was arriving a few hours after me.

The airport was, as usual, quiet. I spotted Lulu / Charles Gilles right away.

I was glad that he had sent me a picture to prepare me, even though when I got it I cried. Several times. But at least the fact that he was bald and wearing an eye patch didn't surprise me.

He had called me just before the Fringe. "This is your mother . . . I have some good news and some bad news."

Given the option, I will always choose the good news first.

"I'm getting married to Billy. Tomorrow."

"Oh my god—congratulations! But I thought that was supposed to be sometime next year. Besides, how can you possibly get married without your Royal Daughter the First present?"

"Well . . . that's the bad news. I have a brain tumour. So we're doing it now."

A few words . . . and everything changed.

THE RADIATION treatment seemed like nothing compared to the experience of the waiting room of the cancer ward. It's more like a small community than a group of patients. They all share a powerful bond. And the cookies get passed around every ten minutes. I dip my sixth Oreo in my coffee and leaf through a magazine.

When his name is called, I follow him into the radiation room. The machine is huge and dominates the space. He looks small lying on the giant tray that holds patients in place. The nurses, all of whom read Lulu's blog and know all about her Halifax drag career, are extremely friendly and welcoming . . . but unlike Lulu's new husband, I am asked to leave while the machine runs its course. I think of making a joke about how I'm her Sister, and that must count as Family, but head outside for a smoke instead.

Later, we walk through the Public Gardens downtown, taking pictures of everything. Lulu teaches me the "Tyra" style of group self-portraits: holding the camera above you and looking up, thus eliminating any possibility of jowls or double chins sneaking into the shot. Valuable advice for Queens in their forties.

I tell Lulu about one of my favourite Halifax memories: ten years earlier, on our first trip east, Kevin and I were walking along the waterfront. It was morning, and it was foggy. I heard accordion music wafting through the mist, but it wasn't your standard oompah-Canadian accordion; it was haunting. Gypsy-ish. European. I followed the sounds, and there she was . . . an old lady with fingerless gloves, playing an old button accordion. I stood there frozen. Not only was the music beautiful, the minor keys floating through the fog, but so was she. The picture was perfect. I wished I had a camera. I memorized the moment, storing it for later.

Ten years later, I ask Lulu about the old lady. I desperately want to see her again and get some pictures this time.

"She died . . . a few years ago. It was front page news. She was an institution."

I am crushed. All those times I meant to get back to Halifax, and didn't . . . now wishing I had tried harder. But then I am thrilled that at least I got to see her, hear her music, just that once. I realize, again, how lucky I am to at least see it once.

THE FIRST show that Lulu did after her chemo and radiation treatments started was the talk of the town. The billboard outside Reflections read, simply: LULU'S BACK!

As Lulu gets in drag at home, she decides to shave off her

eyebrows, since they'll inevitably fall out eventually anyway. Her skin is fabulous and baby-smooth—one of the upsides of having most of your hair fall out. As an added gimmick, she chooses three gowns for the evening that have scrap material left over. She spends a few minutes at the kitchen table, cutting out sequined fabric and attaching it to the eyepatches she has to wear in order to prevent balance issues.

The crowd is delirious that she's back. Lulu opens the show wearing some seriously high heels that she bought online from Frederick's, and the most complicated outfit I've seen in a long time. She later wisely changes into something a bit more partially-blind-friendly. When she performs "Cotton Fields," complete with lip-synched yodelling, the audience literally starts square dancing.

I've never seen anything quite like it. Wait, yes I have . . . every time she performed. Well, except for the square dancing.

ONE NIGHT in Halifax, I get to see the local Queens strut their stuff. It's always amazing to me, to see the whole story being played out again and again wherever I go. There's me . . . there's Lulu . . . there's Neon . . . ahh, and I see Twiggy. Not us, but the new versions of us, twenty years later. The characters stay the same, even if the names and outfits change. The story we lived, and thought was so unique, has not only been lived and played out a million times since, but was ages old by the time we lived it. Youth are always arrogant enough to think that what they are experiencing is so unusual, so different from the lives of everyone else. I think back to the day I first read Quentin Crisp, and realized that he had beaten me to every "original" thought and experience I had ever had.

Lulu receives an award that night . . . it's presented by the Empress, but it's from the Mayor of Halifax. Even the unflappable Lulu is blown away by the honour.

ONE NIGHT I go to one of the Halifax bars for a beer. I sit alone on the patio where I can smoke. The bartender and I start chatting about the drag scene. I ask him what he thinks of the girls. He tells me that none of them has even come close to Lulu.

"Yeah, she's pretty amazing, isn't she?" I ask.

"Yeah. You know, they wrote a book about her," he says.

"Yeah, I heard," I laugh, and I realize that in Halifax, *The Edmonton Queen* isn't a book by Darrin Hagen, but a book about Lulu LaRude.

FLYING HOME, I cruise the channels on the plane, looking for something to distract me from the long flight. I stumble on some local show, the kind they film live at noon, with local issues and guests. There is a handsome man giving makeup tips to callers. I watch for a good five minutes, wondering where I know this guy from, when I suddenly hear a familiar laugh. It's Chuck. He's healthy, has all his hair and eyebrows, and looks like a million bucks.

I can't believe how quickly the new picture of him has pushed the old one out of my head.

WHEN I talk to Lulu on the phone, to ask her about the new edition of the book, she sometimes sounds tired. I always try to ask how she's feeling, but never know what to say if the answer isn't good. It sometimes feels like I'm pestering her . . . the curious daughter peppering the exhausted mother with question after question. It almost feels like this is the only chance I will ever have to tell her how important she is to me. And then, I realize that I've already done that with the first book. And it's probably selfish to hope for two chances like that in one lifetime.

IRIS BUYS Lulu a plane ticket to Edmonton to do a show as a fundraiser for Loud & Queer. It is Lulu's 25th Anniversary of doing drag. We call it the Anniversary Tour. Lulu is joined on stage by Twiggy, Neon, and two brilliant newcomers: Bianca and Vanity Fair. Everyone asks why I'm not in drag to perform with Lulu.

"Because," I answer, "this is the drag show I want to watch."

I take pictures and laugh and cheer as the Girls hit the stage at Buddy's Niteclub. At one point, Twiggy and Lulu perform the sign language number that Lulu and I made famous decades ago, the one that is performed by Queens all over North America. The magic, as always, is still there.

I drop Chuck at the airport when the weekend is over. A giant hug, an I love you, and he disappears through the revolving door.

LULU SPENT Christmas in the hospital. She had been feeling a little ragged, but had big plans for her first family holiday with her new hubby, so she had ignored the warnings her body gave her and kept planning for one of her favourite celebrations: the Gillis family Christmas in Cape Breton. A series of complications ended up cancelling the holiday, however. After New Year's, she was back home and feeling great, and sent me her letter for the last chapter of the book, apologizing for delivering it so much later than expected. Again, I felt bad for dragging her repeatedly back to the past while she was dealing with so much in the present.

IT'S GETTING harder every day to write this. I feel like I'm writing a eulogy for someone who's still alive. I'm calling Lulu every other day, trying to track down this photo or that memory. Part of me feels that if I draw this chapter to a close, then that's it. It will be over. And part of me knows that the reason I'm having trouble is that the story is still being written. And no matter how hard I try, I will never really be able to do the experience justice.

THE ORIGINAL deadline for the new material for this book has been delayed . . . several times. Lulu is always on my mind. It's glorious—and exhausting—to be reliving our time together. I try to hurry, to be able to get the writing done before it's over, to visit Lulu and put the new edition of the book in her hands. I go to Vancouver, to visit Cleo, and I promise my publisher that I can deliver the goods by the time I get back.

While I'm there, a message from Kevin that Lulu called, and that I'm to call her back. It's late in Halifax, but I've been waiting to hear whether or not Lulu found the originals of our very first photo shoot: I need them back for the book. Positive that she has located them, I call.

Instead: "I got 'the talk' from my doctor today," she says.

A chill . . . she's been in the hospital pretty often for the last couple of weeks. I'm learning to steel myself for bad news every time we talk.

"I have two months left. Give or take."

Give or take—what? A life? A death? It's cancer, so we've all seen enough television movies and miracle stories to know that two months could translate into four months, or eight months, or longer. The day she sent me a letter for the book, she said she was feeling fabulous. The unpredictability of the ups and downs . . . she seems to swing from one to the other.

She says that if he ever gets sick of being in the hospital, he will just start smoking so they will kick him out and send him home.

I tell her that Cleo and I are going to have lunch at Tallulah's favourite greasy spoon on Denman. She says something about Tallulah getting a space ready for her in whatever afterlife there is. Either that, or she says that Tallulah will tune in whoever is in charge and demand that Lulu get sent back. I'm not sure, as her speech has begun to slur.

She talks, I listen. It's late, and I think she's falling asleep as she talks . . . either that, or I'm not understanding. I listen anyway, just to hear her voice. I wonder if this edition will be done in time for her to see . . . or if this edition is for everyone else.

CLEO AND I go to "The Grove" for lunch. It was where I spent many of my last moments with Tallulah in 1991. We would wake up late (no doubt we had talked into the wee hours the night before), and she would say, "Ready for breakfast?" and we would walk the two blocks to the restaurant.

Somehow, Tallulah's favourite table was always open when we arrived. Maybe they held it for her every day until lunch.

She and I would sit and chat and smoke and smoke and smoke. Her table was in the window, and this being Vancouver's West End at some point every homo and Queen that ever walked Denman would pass by, stop in, visit, and leave. We called it "holding court."

Cleo and I have the clubhouse with fries. Tallulah's table is full, so we sit nearby. Once we are done eating, the other people leave. Cleo and I move to Tallulah's table and get our waitress to take our picture.

In the old days, Lunch With Tallulah would end in time for us to head back to her place for supper. Now, Cleo and I pause for a moment, and think of our friend, and wish she was at the table with us . . .

. . . and that, if we sat there long enough, every one of the friends we had lost would pass by.

AS PLANNED on the morning of February 4, 2007, friends from all over Canada started their day by praying for a miracle. In the frozen wilds of Edmonton, I lit a candle for Lulu. At first, I didn't think it would light . . . it struggled. Then it caught, and the flame rose—calm, serene, perfect, and unmoving. I guess I do believe in miracles, even if I think they come from a different place than many people do.

I go to Chuck's website several times a day, just to see who's left a comment or a word of hope for him. The list is like a who's who of the Canadian scene . . . and yet so many names aren't there. I know everyone has their own way of dealing with tragedy and pain. But I also know that we get very few chances to tell the people we love how much they mean to our lives.

I haven't called him in days, because I know as soon as he posted the news, his home was probably inundated with calls. Friends that I met on my last trip to Halifax send me notes, give me the updates.

BILLY ANSWERED the phone today. Chuck has been moved back into the hospital. They're attempting a new painkiller regime. As I sit in Edmonton—reliving and remembering the old days that I spent with him—his friends and his love and his family are dealing with the day-to-day reality of watching a friend struggle.

On Chuck's website, the messages keep pouring in. People from all over Canada say hello, I'm so sorry, I'll pray and hope for you. Amazing how many lives are touched by one Queen.

His friends huddle close for warmth. Any chance to be close to him now, even if communication is next to impossible, even if his stories blur together, is cherished and held dear. I hear that he is constantly using his hands, "making" things with them. He's imagining it all, of course, but the hands keep "making" things. Who knows what he's creating now . . . a stunning lamp, a new headdress made of tinfoil takeout lids, a brave new world for all the outsiders to take up residence in . . . I wouldn't put any of it past him.

TWO MONTHS becomes ten days. It ends on the morning of February 8, 2007.

The Queen is dead.

Long live the Queens.

IN THE February snow, I think back to the warm September I was in Halifax. Lulu was so excited . . . she had managed to get her hands on a piano. She had wanted to keep it a surprise, but couldn't, and had sent me an email with a picture of it sitting in their living room.

When I got to his place, I sat down and started playing. Day after day, Chuck would putter around, tidying, cleaning, going about his life while I relearned songs that used to be the soundtrack of our early years. Gradually, the songs came back: the Kate, the Rickie, the Bach, the Babs. My fingers, a bit hesitant at first, eventually remembered where to go.

And one day, with the sun streaming in, I feel transported back in time. I hear Chuck humming behind me. The ringing of the piano hangs in the air. I hear him say, "I love that song."

"I know," I reply. And we are nineteen again. And the whole history of the world is before us again. All the possibilities, all the laughs, all the heartbreak . . . all of it is just beginning again.

And I would do it all again. Every second of it.

As complicated as our lives became, it was always simple moments like this one that made me love my time with him. Those moments, and the air of potential that always hovered over us.

And always returning to square one.

Never being afraid to start over.

"The Supper Before Last."

The Queens Have Their Say

WHEN *The Edmonton Queen* "came out" ten years ago, I'm not sure what I expected. Somehow I assumed everyone would be as thrilled as I was to revisit that heady decade with all of its accompanying drama. I soon realized that it was to be much more complicated than that.

Within a few months of its release, my publishers called to say that there was a letter at the office for me. It wasn't, as I hoped, my first fan letter . . . in fact, it was a very heartfelt letter from Ora's drag-daughter, Sadie / Shawn. She took me to task for what had become one of the most-discussed scenes in the book: Ora's funeral. Sadie explained that I had misinterpreted Ora's funeral, and, as the person who had planned the whole thing, she was extremely hurt.

I was crushed. Not only did the letter upset me, but it opened up a whole new mystery: what had actually happened? All those things I had heard—were any of them even true? In writing the book, I had "reported" details that remaining members of the drag world had told me . . . some of those things had even become legend, all part of the swirling mythology that was the story of our past lives.

In writing the story of that part of my life, those mythologies became crucial. There were so many gaps, so many blanks, so much I realized I would probably never know. The same story of missing details could probably be told in every city across the continent.

Oral histories take on a life of their own after a few generations. The original story is still in there somewhere, but the act of creating a story sets it free to become whatever it needs to be. People will tell the stories they need to tell. When Lulu tells her Halifax friends stories of our Big Onion adventures, I notice that she tells the book version of the story, as opposed to what actually happened.

In 1997, I went to Vancouver with a pile of pages. It was my final draft (or so I thought at the time) of the original *Edmonton Queen*. I was determined to get permission from everyone mentioned in the book to use their stage names. Most responded by mail, never asking to read the book or check what I was saying. Only one person said no. I used her stage name anyway. But there were a couple of friends I wanted to visit personally. One of these was Annie, the Nina-Hagen-reincarnate who had terrorized Flashback alongside me in the earliest of our punk delusions.

I showed Annie the one brief reference to her. "So now I'm supposed to sign something without reading the rest of the book?" she asked.

I assured her that I had written it with the best of intentions. "Here. Read the last chapter," I suggested. "You'll get an idea of where I'm going with this."

Then I sat. And she read. I waited, watching her face. She got to the end and closed it. Then she wiped away a tear.

"Well?" I waited for her to tell me that it was beautiful.

Instead, she cleared her throat. "I didn't know Stephen was dead."

I was dumbfounded. She was referring to Iona Box. Iona/Stephen had lived with Lulu and I at the infamous Walla Walla West, and Annie had always been close to him. I went to hug her. In doing so, I knocked over my Pepsi all over her coffee table. We wiped up the spilled drink, both wiping tears as we did. I've always had a way of ruining the moment.

It reminded me of something that had happened in 1995, a year before I ever launched into the experience of writing the book. I was performing at Rebar, an alternative club in Edmonton, when I ran into Stanley Carroll in the kitchen. I hadn't seen him for at least a few years, so we were catching up on old times. Stanley is a prominent designer who I had known since the Flashback years. He and his wife Marcie had designed several outfits for Tallulah in the old days, including the infamous Thunderdome dress.

Suddenly Stanley asked, "How's our old friend?"

"God, which one?"

"Tallulah. I haven't heard from him in years."

My heart broke. At that point, Tallulah / Lou had already been dead for a couple of years. Stanley had been one of Lou's friends all the way back from high school in Yellowknife. And yet, somehow, he hadn't heard. And I had to tell him. And all the pain flooded back again.

At the time, it seemed like one of those things that could only happen once. And yet, over the next few years, it happened again and again.

In writing the original *Edmonton Queen*, I had come up against similar gaps in information . . . either no one knew the answer to my questions, or there was no one to ask, or a legend which I had assumed was true because I had heard it so many times just turned out to be juicy gossip. Mix that with moments that are misinterpreted through the veil of grief, or moments that even now are too painful for some people to talk about, and it becomes easier to see how "truths" can vary according to the storyteller.

WHEN I started phoning some of the girls for comments on the original book to expand the 10th anniversary edition, or for comments on that crazy time, I wasn't completely convinced that it was a good idea. Many of the Queens from those years aren't doing drag anymore . . . some will never step into a dress again. And the one thing I learned when the book first came out was that not everyone from that world was as eager to revisit those memories as I was. But I did know that there were things that definitely needed clarification, and that some of the girls were the only ones who could offer that. I also knew that, despite my best intentions, mine was only one version of the story. It was time to give the girls a say . . . even the ones who weren't happy with what I wrote in the first place.

Some of the Queens in the book were extremely relieved to only be mentioned fleetingly. Others were upset that they were not mentioned at all. I have had friends tell me they have no intention of ever buying the book because they lived it. And there are those who were so upset that I went back to that time at all that they will never speak to me again. There are Queens who were upset and got over it; there are those who said they were fine and then trashed me all over town.

And there are Queens who love the book, and appreciate the history it attempts to recover, proudly showing it off to their new friends as a way of showing where they come from.

It was a time that was as magical as it was desperate and frightening; even as we lived it, we knew that it was unique. And everyone who went through it has a different reaction to being reminded of those years. Some can't let go of those years; others have buried it forever.

This isn't an attempt to set the record straight, because there is no one singular truth here. This is, after all, a fairy tale, a collective mythology. Every one of the Queens mentioned here played a part, whether by design or by accident.

Mandy Kamp / Mark was in many early Guys In Disguise productions, and jumped at the chance to be in the first play version of *The Edmonton Queen* in 1996. We used her as a "shadow portrait" on stage. She learned the moves of the Queens in the play, bringing them to life as live silhouettes. She later moved and became the toast of Vancouver, eventually crowned as Empress. Minutes after I ran into her on a Vancouver sidewalk, she wrote:

> *Dear Darrin,*
> *I have never been so honoured to be a part of something so special.*
> *Performing behind that scrim in* The Edmonton Queen—*the play—portraying some of our beloved*

sisters was an experience that was truly magical. Also being the first drag queen to be at the Sterling Awards when you won that year for the play was indeed memorable.

Thank you for allowing me to be involved with this project and thank you so much for telling our story.

Now, to the dirt. First of all, I have learned that Grindl *didn't* die under a table. When I first learned this, I was actually almost sad, because Grindl's famous last scene was already legend when I moved to Edmonton. Word from Chatty Cathy Jackson and Lindee Star is that Grindl, who did love partying under tables at the various clubs around town, was extremely difficult to wake up one night at a party . . . so difficult, in fact, that she was sent to the hospital later in the evening, where she never really recovered from whatever had knocked her down, and died a few days later.

I have to admit, I was actually disappointed to find out the truth. More upset than I, was Lulu, who loved telling that legend. It was one of those juicy pieces of gossip that seemed to fit the rules of our new world: die young, stay pretty. And in that time, the act of drag was not just a proclamation of self, but an act of defiance, sometimes with ultimate consequences.

Some lived through the experience and have used the lessons learned in those years to build a new beginning for themselves.

Cleo / Berend, Mz. Flashback 13, is now an actor in Vancouver. He now only does drag if it's for an acting role. He can be seen in *Catwoman*, playing the femmy-guy-at-the-next-office-cubicle. Cleo's story in the book was told pretty much exactly how it happened.

That whole time of my life is awash in memories full of love, laughter, and living. I think what you captured best in the book is each character's desire to live life fully in the moment, good or bad, and to be as fabulous as we knew God had made us to be . . . even if the world around us was telling us otherwise.

I think often of the loved ones we have lost over the past twenty years. People like Lulu, Tallulah and Ora Fice, Excretia and Millie, each in their own brave way helped make the world an easier place for me to live in. Because of them I have grown into a proud gay man, drag queen, brother, son, and friend.

I think what your book does is shows us how far we have come and that those who came before us should never be forgotten.

There are things I wish I would have written differently as well. For example, Mrs. K. and Lindee Star were two extremely important figures in my early drag days . . . the book reduces them to "Old Guard" and sets Lulu and I in direct opposition to them. In reality, I remember the night I was dancing alone on the speaker to "It's Raining Men" and saw Mrs. K. watching me. She offered me my first spot in my first show. And it was Lindee Star who transformed me into the Nubian Goddess I needed to be for what was to be my drag debut—the Black and White Dreams show.

My official drag debut came on January 14, 1983. One drag show under my belt, and I thought I knew it all. In fact, I was cocky enough to do a photo shoot the next day for a friend of mine from high school who was taking a design course. The next day found me hung over and, frankly, pretty skanky looking in Churchill Station, posing for the camera. I couldn't figure out for the life of me how to do my makeup again. I hadn't paid any attention as it was going on; I just knew that it had taken hours. It would take me years to develop a decent technique in that department. I quickly learned that drag wasn't as easy as the girls made it look. Somewhere there is a picture of me by a sign that says, "Slippery when wet." Trust me: slippery was the least of my problems on that photo shoot.

In the oversimplification that is necessary to write a clear story, Mrs. K. and Lindee became peripheral characters.

Mrs. K. / Mr. K. / Gerry writes (with tongue planted firmly in cheek):

> *I did so enjoy reading your little* roman à clef *when it was issued all those years ago.*
>
> *But I thought I'd take the opportunity to drop the tiniest of notes, just to clarify the very smallest of omissions in your original. Knowing me as you do, I'm sure you'll realize that I mean not a word of critique—just working hard as ever to ensure an accurate historical representation.*
>
> *I did just want to point out my surprise at the minimalist way you presented the influence I had on your fledgling career. So like you, to understate the enormity and depth of influence I wielded to point your toes on the path to stardom. But this anniversary edition presents the ideal opportunity for you to clarify how I led you, Svengali-like, before the footlights. No need to mention the costs I incurred on your behalf, or the injurious impact on my own career. That's just all water under the bridge, n'est pas?*
>
> *I, like your readers, long to hear the corrected stories of days gone by, when you and I trod the boards. I was by your side, and yet you spoke so briefly of our shared triumphs in your little treatise.*

Mrs. K. is absolutely right on some counts . . . before I met Lulu and we became fast friends, Mrs. K. and Lindee Star took me under their wings. They were still very much in the picture when I ran for Mz. Flashback in 1984. Mrs. K. became Mr. K. and ran alongside me for the Mr. Title. In the photo shoot for my Mz. Flashback campaign, we got dressed in the most bizarre neo-new-wave drag possible and headed to Churchill Square. Mr. K. and I ended up becoming Mr. and Mz. Flashback IX (thanks to Yoda, the midget). Mrs. K. was far from Old Guard . . . her reign as Empress walked a fine balance between madness and the truly bizarre. It was Mrs. K. who wouldn't let Lulu and I back out of our first public photo shoot: the Salute to Trailer Court Women, when we dressed in Value Village cast-offs from the attic of Walla Walla West, piled into a couple of cars and headed for several trailer courts around the city. Following the old adage, "it's easier to ask for forgiveness than permission," we set up camp on several trailer doorsteps and took pictures. The day ended with us heading to the Legislature fountain (our favourite, and the site of many rituals), and getting out of drag in the fountain in front of hundreds of families sunning on a Saturday afternoon.

When it came to my year as Mz. Flashback, I'm glad there were no video cameras for the most part. I was a good performer, but a lousy organizer. When I really hit my stride was in Tallulah's year, by which point I had bullied my way into organizing everything to make the reigning Mz. look consistently fabulous. Mrs. K. left me to my own devices for the entire year, as she had already had her fill of drag pageantry during her year as Empress VIII. But, as a gift to me, she offered to make me my stepping-down gown. Mrs. K. had a way with a sewing machine, so this was indeed a welcome offer. We decided our theme would be "Party in Paisley," meaning I needed a paisley gown. We found some material I could afford, but it was destined to be a modest gown. "Unless," Mrs. K. said, "we can get our hands on a bolt of crinoline."

"A whole bolt? How much will that cost?"

"A lot. But if we got a whole bolt, we could make an amazing pouf at the bottom of the dress."

"I can't afford that."

"I know. But I have an idea . . ."

The next day I was crouched behind a counter in a fabric store, panicking as I tried to stuff an entire bolt of red crinoline into my duffle bag as Mrs. K. kept the lone saleslady busy with question after inane question. It took forever, but at last I rushed out of the store with my prize. Back at Mrs. K.'s, we unfolded the bolt to thread and bunch it for the gown. It stretched three whole city lots. When assembled, the giant pouf at the bottom of the dress was EPIC. The gown was fabulous.

Lindee and Mrs. K. fussed over me in the drag room. My hair, which was now long enough to wear without wiggage, was piled in a tousled beauteousness, poking through the crown, set fetchingly on my head. A last piece of red crinoline (to match the pouf on the bottom of the dress) was added as a final splash of fabulousness. The Mz. Flashback banner, which had been through hell and was looking a little ragged, was draped on me and I was ready. That night I looked as glamorous as I ever had. The dress was fabulous. And, by the end of my Stepping-Down number, completely ruined by the Life Brand cereal that Millie had dumped on me.

These years were important for Lindee Star / Ross. She was Empress when I moved to Edmonton, and had nurtured a healthy respect from her constituents. She parlayed this into her business, now an enormously successful salon. It was Lindee who wrote an article, defending the art of drag and the dignity of its practitioners, in one of the early Queer magazines that attempted to get a foothold in Edmonton.

When Lindee heard from me in regard to the anniversary edition, she wasn't at all sure how to respond.

> *There is a phone message on my desk and my Executive Assistant sticks her head in my office and reminds me to call a Darrin Hagen. It's about some Edmonton Queen or other. I think to myself as I pick up the phone Darrin, Darrin, Dar . . . Gloria! I immediately put down the phone and begin the long familiar wrestle with myself. Do I want to call? Do I want to get involved? Should I just let it rest?*

Lindee's initial reluctance isn't unique . . . but call me she did, and in our conversation we discussed whether or not the book strays too far from the truth. Lindee had recently experienced the thrill of receiving the DVD of the old Flashback shows that she had starred in . . . and then the heartbreak of watching it and realizing that it might still be too soon to go back to that time, even in memory, even for a moment.

This time was a time of creative pretend, a time where I could act out a lot of ideas and behaviours that I could never have allowed Ross to play out. Lindee Star however was always allowed . . . pretty much to do anything she pleased. I learned a lot from her. After years of this kind of club play I had had enough success (and did Darrin and I mention "applause"?), to put aside the tool that was Lindee Star and start to create under my own name, my own persona.

I could never have been successful in my life if it hadn't been for the drag, the acceptance, the "finally being on the inside instead of the outside." The power that comes with being popular and attended cannot be overlooked.

During our phone call Darrin asked me if I felt ashamed, to which I replied "No, never!" In actual fact, creating Lindee Star was one of the first adult successes I had in my life.

I feel grateful for this time but I also feel a great sense of loss. So many people I have loved are no longer with us. Any kind of touch into this "world gone by" is a sharp reminder of that loss. I guess I still feel the pain acutely. One so young should not have to endure so much loss. It changes you. It changed me.

Back to the question at hand: did Darrin recall these events accurately? Absolutely! I just remembered them differently. I needed to.

Twiggy was very helpful when I was writing the book the first time around . . . not only to clarify events, timelines and details, but because, next to Neon, she had the biggest treasure trove of drag photos and archives. At some point, friends like Twiggy and Neon must have been praying for me to just release the damn book and stop pestering them. Ten years later, I find myself calling them up one more time and asking them to repeat the whole process of locating photos. In spite of my decades of harassment, Twiggy writes:

> I must admit, while you were in the process of writing "the book" and calling me about dates, people, circumstances, photos, and general recollections, I had mixed emotions about the endeavour. Not to say that I thought you would fail or anything like that, I guess I was envious, maybe even jealous that I hadn't done it first!!! After all, I was there too . . .
>
> Frankly, I'm too damn lazy and I don't own a laptop.
>
> I did have so much fun filling in some of the blanks and reliving some outrageous and hilarious memories as well as the painful tragic ones. But, a small part of our lives is forever in print. I'm thrilled to be a minor celebrity in a major book!
>
> I'm so happy to still be a part of your life and you in mine. I'm so very proud of you (all jealousy aside). I would like to congratulate you on this anniversary of The Edmonton Queen, NOT a Riverboat Story and look so forward to reading the rest of the letters from everyone, even the bitter ones!

I was googling my name one day (I know, that sounds vain, but I do it regularly to keep abreast of what's written about me), and one of the links took me to a Flickr webpage. Flickr is an online phenomenon where photography addicts post and enjoy photos. *The Edmonton Queen* was listed under someone's profile as their favourite book. Apparently, like me and so many others, Trash / Terry had found his way there and was posting photos of his rock sculptures on English Bay. Trash's public art has been viewed, enjoyed, and photographed by thousands. The way both Trash and I explored our feelings of loss manifested itself in very differently, and yet the intent was identical: to memorialize the people we miss.

> *My dearest Gloria:*
>
> *Today is yesterday's tomorrow and will be tomorrow's yesterday.*
>
> *I have just finished reading* The Edmonton Queen *again and thought I would let you know that there is just too much about you and not enough about me.*
>
> *Every time I have read your book it fills me with so many emotions that my mind goes into overdrive thinking about all the fabulous people that have been in my life. You have put into printed word the story of a family that in sooooooo many ways was just like any NORMAL family.*
>
> *But ours was unique, wasn't it?*
>
> *Some of the stories are not as I remember them, but we each have our own way of looking at our family and remembering people and situations. It is no different than when I sit with my sisters and brothers and talk about our childhood . . . we all have different versions of what really happened and yet we are all right as we were all there.*
>
> *Flashback and all the people there will always be a huge part of my soul and I am a better person for being a part of this family. You are and always will be one of my best friends and I wish for you and all my sisters everything good life has to offer.*
>
> > *All my love to those I love.*
> > *I am and always will be . . . TRASH*

The works of art inspired by the Edmonton Queens doesn't stop there: Gretchen Wilder / David commissioned an artist to gather together the old girls' Club one more time. The result is "The Supper Before Last," a revisiting of Leonardo's masterpiece, but starring the Empress Club of Edmonton. When

I asked Gretchen what had prompted the piece, she explained that Jesus was a rebel. And when the religious right uses Jesus to justify injustice, it denies the purpose of his rebellion. "The way I see it," she explained, "if Jesus was on earth today, he would be sitting down to dinner with drag queens. That's the kind of statement he would make: rebellious, against the grain, but ultimately logical and right." That, mixed with the desire to see the Girls collected one more time as a group, brought another piece of art into the world. "Ultimately, I did it for me," Gretchen added.

There are people in the book who aren't Queens, but lived the same hard and fast life that the Queens did. In the world of Flashback, they found the same acceptance and friendship as the Queens, but were often pushed aside in the swirl of glitter and ego that was our life. Right by our side was Neon, Den Mother Ultima, performing with us, sharing our laughs and loves.

It's hard to believe it was so long ago. Some of the things seem like yesterday. The memories and experiences can be crisp and clear, soft and blurry or even tearful and painful. All of it is beautiful. We were so fortunate to be a part of that place at that time. It has shaped who we have become, for good or for bad.

This year is also the 20th anniversary of Twiggy and my reign as Mr. and Mz. Flashback 11. In our usual bizarre way, at this time Twiggy and I are roommates, living in apartment #11. We've lived a lifetime since then and yet find ourselves still connected by coincidences. As much as we may want to try to get away from it, we are all a product of our upbringing. It's all a huge Flashback.

I wish we could all live in the humour of it. We had a lot of fun, folks. Please remember that first. We were blessed by whatever forces you believe or don't believe in. At least we were there. Now we are here to remember and recount it. The thing that I think

*Darrin did through this book was give **his** voice to those of us who aren't here anymore. Whether you believe it to be the truth or not, he has immortalized them. I have had complete strangers talk to me about Tallulah and Ora and everyone else in the book. It makes my heart happy to know that anyone can know that these incredible people lived.*

We are the generation that suffered the awful consequences of the worst plague in the world. Like some kind of veterans from a holocaust, we are still dealing with the ramifications. I think it's our duty to keep fighting the fight. Send the message out. Whether it is through reaching out to those affected or by writing a tender account of it all. Our voices need to be heard, and these stories were told with humour and drama.

I remember whining at Darrin about my lack of story in the book. I remember him telling me to write my own book. These stories are his. I agree.

If you disagree, write your own book.

I remain,
Neon

Two of the saddest stories for me are Tallulah's and Ora's. Part of the pain comes from knowing I will never have a chance to tell them how important they were . . . are . . . to me. And still more pain comes from the reactions their stories inspired in friends who were even closer to them than I was.

One line I removed from this edition of the book was a single line about the last days of Tallulah. I used to say, "She died angry." But the years have shown me that, like many other claims, that one was totally subjective. My last days with Tallulah were at least two years away from her actual last days. And one person who was with Tallulah / Lou in her near-to-last days was her friend Shelley, an '80s party girl for whom Flashback and its denizens were a release from a life of negativism and self-censorship. Shelley wrote:

I spent Lou's last Christmas and New Year's with him, his partner, and his family. His parents, Grandmother, and Uncle had come to spend the holidays with him. It made for interesting times, as the only one who could speak English was his Uncle. But, the more time I spent with them, the more I realized it didn't matter. We were all there for Lou.

When I was there, he would go into these fevers and be wracked with pain. The morphine helped, but not totally. His Grandmother, Mother, and I would sit on the couch, feeling totally helpless. We would watch as his partner tried to make him as comfortable as possible and help him through the pain. I would try not to cry, but sometimes I would. Lou's mom would reach across, squeeze my hand, and smile knowingly. Now I know where he got his strength from.

His Grandmother and Mother cooked up enough food to feed the entire West End over the holidays. I must have gained 10 pounds when I was there. I would sit beside Lou and he would point out all his favourite dishes from his childhood, while his Mother and Grandmother piled our plates up.

Even though he knew he didn't have much longer, he didn't dwell on it. He was so happy to be surrounded by the people he loved. No bitterness, just contentment, love, and peace.

One of the hardest things I've had to do was say goodbye to Lou that last day. I knew there would be no more vacations to Vancouver to see him, no staying up all hours talking and giggling, no wieners wrapped in bread with mustard (one of Lou's favourites).

He died that February.

Not many people knew, but I would not be here if it wasn't for Lou. I can truthfully say he actually saved my life.

I still have his letters and I have read them

*numerous times over the years. I still miss him and I
still love him. No regrets.*

Sometimes, the myth that sprang up in the absence of truth
didn't come close to being anywhere as fantastic as what actually
happened.

One of the Queens who got the roughest ride in the book
was Iris. Since the book came out, I have always been surprised
at how easily she forgave the mean jabs and stories I brought
up about her. Just like in the Flashback days, Iris is pretty
unflappable, proving that we always sold her short when it came
to giving her credit for her talents. And for her survival skills.

Iris never complained once about my portrayal of her, and
if anyone had a reason to complain, it was Iris. When she and
I finally reconnected after all those years, we actually got along
better than we ever had in the old days. And so I asked Iris to
tell the real story of why she was arrested that night in the drag
room so many years ago. Once more, the truth ended up being
more fantastic than anything I could have invented.

*The whole fish tank thing: well, the tank didn't
belong to Lori St. John, and I didn't sell it. Lori and
her friend C____ (the tank was his), involved me in
a little credit card theft (that I didn't know about),
and got me arrested with C____ (Lori slipped out a
side door before the cops got there). This was when
Lori and I lived together as roommates in the Avord
Arms. I worked at a salon in the day, and the clubs
at night. Lori was in and out of the hospital for his
diabetes. He'd go in every so often and have a couple
of toes off. Anyway, Lori and C____ thought it
would be a good idea to steal a credit card from the
guy in the next bed while he was out of the room
for tests. Later that day C____ called me at work
to see if I could meet him and Lori, to go help them
pick out a stereo for the apartment. C____ had been*

staying with us for a while, and I thought he was trying to be nice. He'd told me he'd got a new job a few days earlier. So off we went. By 8 pm I was in custody with C_____ and Lori had slithered away. By 8 am I was released after hours of being grilled, and accused of masterminding the whole thing (ya right!). C_____ had confessed to the whole thing sometime during the night, and I'd given up the only info I could which was where Lori might be hiding. And yes, I ratted her out!

The cops picked Lori up at the apartment. By the time she got out "scott free" I'd been up for about 36 hours, 24 with no food, but I had managed to smoke a whole pack of cigs before Lori got home around noon. As the door to the apartment opened I went off like Krakatoa! For more than a hour I spat my venom at him, not even giving him a chance to reply. Then I got dressed and left for work (I was crabby!).

When I got home I started packing, and wasn't speaking to Lori. A few days into this I got a call from C_____, apologizing for what had happened and to see if his things were safe. Lori had pawned most of his things: all that was left were his fish tank and a pile of pawn tickets. I had been taking care of the fish, so he asked me if I would keep on taking care of them till he got out of jail. I said I would and hung up.

At this point I really needed a break from the city, so I sold my furniture, left the fish tank with a friend, and went back to Grande Prairie. The next time I saw Lori St. John was at the Entertainer of the Year show at Flashback that fall. Lori took her chance to get revenge, called the cops, and told them I had stolen the tank from her. She'd told them that the furniture was hers too, but then I had the receipts *for what I had sold. They still decided to believe that the tank was his, and I was lying about everything. I told them that the tank belonged to C_____ and when he got out I'd do my best to get it back to him. I told them where to find it, and so they went and got it, flushed about $1500.00 worth of tropical fish and took the tank into evidence.*

From what then should have been a civil matter, and handled in the lower courts, the Judge decided he didn't want to be bothered with such a foolish case and bumped it up to Court of Queen's Bench. So now I'm facing ten years in jail! I defended myself for two years, spent thousands of dollars . . . all because I called Lori St. John a thieving, pizza-licking trash bag (which she was)!

In the end, all of the prosecution's witnesses told the same story as I had. The jury acquitted me and the new judge apologized to me for what had happened to me, and that it was unfortunate that Lori could not be countercharged for his wrongdoing (he was on AISH); as a ward of the government I couldn't have him charged. Then the judge gave the prosecuting attorney a dressing down (I was still too shocked to giggle). It looked good on the bitch!

And I walked out, free of Lori St. John's toxic presence. Lori eventually wound up having more and more cut off and died. Karma really can bite!

OXOX Iris Shopashinski

I feel the need to take a moment here to redeem Lori St. John's reputation. I am sure the story Iris tells about the fish tank debacle is true. But every Queen has her moment of shining in a spotlight.

For Lori St. John, that moment was the day she recognized a murderer while cruising on The Hill. The suspect had come to the Club the night before, taken home Copa, one of our friends and a waiter at Flashback. The next morning we got the call that Copa was dead, stabbed in the heart with one of the knives from his kitchen cupboard. The very next night Lori, who had seen the two of them leave together, saw him cruising, probably for victim number two. Rather than run, she pretended to buy his services for the night, took him for breakfast at the Dapple Grey Café, ordered him bacon and eggs, excused herself for a moment, and called the police. They arrested him minutes later. Lori's act of bravery got her a special award from the Empress that year. The murderer got seven years for manslaughter.

This pull between good and evil, between callousness and compassion, seems to be behind the split personality of so many Queens. When I finally spoke with Ora's drag-daughter Sadie, in an attempt to address the initial telling of the funeral story, the first thing we agreed on was that Ora / Kyle was both someone we had loved, and someone who we could never trust. We have so many fond memories of her, and just as many that still make us furious when we think about how she manipulated people.

I asked her what lines, in particular, she wanted me to address. I told her to grab her copy. She told me that she had thrown it out shortly after reading it, that she had been so excited to finally show her mother and her grandmother why Flashback and the Sisterhood had meant so much to her, but that she couldn't, because they would have been as hurt as she was about my claims of Ora dying alone.

And so I forwarded her the original text. The next day, I got this letter.

I finished the whole book last night and can now recall how furious I was about the sum-up of Kyle's passing because I am again.

The Flashback family were his only family at the end!!!!! What a crock of shit!! I'm sure most of the people who did show up just wanted to make sure he WAS dead!!

Funny how none of his "family" bought flowers,

or offered to help with the funeral expenses . . . I guess it was just more convenient being "family" when he was footing the bill or handing out loans to people that he loved (and thought loved him in return).

My grandmother spoke to him weekly on the phone. Every month, every birthday, Valentine's, Easter, and Christmas he was treated as if he was a grandson, and sent cards and gifts.

He was cremated with a teddy bear that Nan had given him (Costa). Kyle made me promise that I would. The nurse had even put a toe tag on the bear to make sure the crematorium would do the job.

He was NOT dead when I found him in the apartment . . . in fact I held his hand in the trauma unit while they cut open his throat to put in a tube so he could breathe.

By then most people at the hospital knew me. For two years I was there when he woke up after each procedure. I sat through all the consults, the meds that didn't work, the dementia, his first heart attack, finding him in his apartment in a coma, taking over the wheel of the car because he would have to save whatever he was spitting up at the time to show his doctor, getting calls at all hours because for two whole years my life revolved around helping Kyle Edgar die. Did I mention he was afraid of needles, so every day before work I'd have to go to his apartment and give him his chemo . . . nope, no Flashback "family" there!!

And finally, yes, he was alive when I found him. He had had a heart attack and several strokes but he was very much alive. I spent the night with him in trauma holding his hand because his brain was so fried all he could SCREAM was my name . . . sorry, nobody from Flashback.

They sliced him open right in front of me, while a nurse held me so that Kyle couldn't see I was fainting, he would only let me wash the dried up puke out of his mouth, I'd been doing it for so long.

After he was stabilized he was moved to ward 7D . . . nobody leaves 7D.

His last words to me in trauma were: "You know what to do" and "I love you" . . . and by the time he had been cleaned up and moved to the ward he was in a coma. The nurse said his heart was so damaged he wouldn't last the night, they moved a bed into the room for me. I didn't stay I had to get home . . . Nan was on her way.

Gord and I got to the airport, got Nan, and checked her into the Century Plaza (right across from the hospital).

We rushed to the ward . . . there was a yellow sticker on his room door telling me to report to the nurse's station . . . I'm not stupid, this time there was nobody to hold me up, I fainted. They asked if I wanted to see him a last time, I said no, just make sure Costa was with him . . . she put on the toe tag.

I got us ready to fly home.

WE sat in the family section of the chapel. In the parking lot at the end of the service I was at the trunk of my Mother's car. I had asked a few people who had given things to Kyle over the years if they wanted a small memento from his apartment. I handed these out to David, Yvette Choma, and Cloretta. Only one person actually offered to buy any of Ora's drag, and that was Mandy Kamp. So out of the trunk came the ONLY piece of drag I brought and I GAVE it to her (we're still in touch, as a matter of fact I saw Mark tonight). There was no sale of anything, no wigs, no glitter, no drag, just one dress to the one person who was decent enough to offer to pay for it. The rest was "lost," but who cares, it was just drag.

That's the way it happened: he wasn't alone. For

two years we were joined at the hip, and he did have
a family that loved him and wanted him home every
chance he got . . . my Nan and Mom.

  I don't want to talk about this anymore tonight.
It still makes me cry.

Shawn

The day after sending this letter, Sadie / Shawn sent me another one apologizing for unleashing ten years' worth of anger in one note. I feel lucky that I finally got to hear what he went through . . . and what Ora went through. Ora was lucky to have family at the end. As much as the letter hurt, I was suddenly happy to know that there was someone there through it all. Family is more than what you're born into; it's who you choose to be with in your life . . .

I left part of the funeral scene in the Ora eulogy, because it's what I thought was happening at the time. I edited out some other details that, in retrospect, I had no right to include. I print Sadie's letter here in its entirety to give him the chance to set his part of the record straight.

Creation comes with a certain responsibility.

AFTER LULU'S funeral, her hubby Billy gave me her copy of *The Edmonton Queen*. I had lost my first copy of the book years ago. But Lulu's copy had managed to keep returning to her, regardless of how many times she lent it to friends. It was worn, ragged, and much-loved, like a favourite teddy bear. It is now one of my most cherished possessions. The dedication reads "To the *Other* Edmonton Queen—This book says pretty much everything I have to say, except: none of this would have happened without you. Now let's get famous!" In the decade that followed the publication of the original edition, that's exactly what happened.

It is my honour to leave the final word to my Dragmother, Lulu LaRude / Charles McDuff Gillis. For the record, I rarely leave the last word to anyone. But it seems right to step aside and let the Legend finally speak. Lulu sent me this letter shortly after New Year's Day, after getting out of the hospital (where she spent much of the holidays). She was still confident that she would beat the cancer, but in reality, she was living the last month of her remarkable life. It is the last email I ever received from her.

> *Well, I am finally free!! Hooray! I feel 100% better than I did a week ago today so needless to say I am happy as a clam!*
>
> *It was funny that earlier today (almost as soon as I was released from the hospital), Flora called and we had a great conversation reminiscing about the old days. We were enjoying a chuckle over one of my fave tales: the night that Flora and I roller-skated home in 40 below weather wearing nothing but bumblebee outfits and using rhinestone turkey basters as microphones interviewing people in the Mac's store. We were both loaded and Flora was sporting a huge bloody knee and shredded pantyhose that she acquired when she wiped out under the train trestle at 109 street. Neon still has pictures of Flora back home laying in the tub—still in the bumblebee outfit with her really scabby bleeding knee hanging over the edge. My god, that was a funny night . . . and I am so glad we were insane enough to make such crazy memories. We were fortunate to make many of them.*
>
> *Darrin, I can't begin to tell you how flattered and touched I was by your incredibly moving dedication. It was truly the most special moment I had ever shared with a friend . . . especially one I had so much professional respect for. I was also thrilled that the "Lulu story" was the seed that grew into* The Edmonton Queen *(even though it wasn't really true). Other than that initial story, the rest of the tales were taken directly from people's lives and were, without a doubt, non-fiction.*

I was drawn in immediately, this flood of wonderful memories of those I had not thought of in ages and the wild and fun times we had. When friends read the book for the first time, they always comment on how insane it was. I can see how people could construe it as fiction, as these stories are truly crazy. But we know the truth. We lived them!!

It was fascinating, as there were many situations that we really didn't discuss at the time. There was a tough time when we were definitely drifting apart . . . and after reading your account of how this happened, I was not surprised to learn that we shared the same ideals at that time. We had different ambitions —and there can only be one leader. It was bound to happen and I held nothing but respect for you during the whole process. You were a creative dynamo who was coming out of his cocoon ready to take on the world, and I was a beautiful showgirl who wanted to be covered in sparkle doing shows in clubs. We both got to do exactly what we wanted to do. I moved to Toronto and found a great life with a pro drag troupe. I was living my dream! You were burgeoning forth with a soon to be widely popular and accomplished career as an award-winning everything. We should have been celebrating our mutual successes. My only regret is that we couldn't find it within us to share that. Realizing we really wanted different things would have opened the doors for so much mutual support. We both made a slight misstep there, but nothing could ever prevent us from being friends. I could never live without my Glo!! I believed then and believe even more after twenty-five years that you are truly one of the most gifted and insanely talented human beings I have ever been honoured with knowing. To know how you feel about me moves me immensely.

Anyway back to The Book! I read it seven times

in two months time . . . laughing, crying, bringing back almost-forgotten memories to centre stage once again . . . filling my head with joy, and my heart with sadness. I lived those stories, and to see them so vividly recalled made me realize that to be presented with a huge document celebrating the most exciting moments in your life is truly the best gift anyone could ever offer. And not just to me, but to everyone honoured in the book. It's simply the best. No gift like it.

You are special in so many ways and I am proud to call you my best friend, my daughter and my brother in the real world. I love you so much and congrats on the anniversary.

Love as always . . . Lu

Darrin and Chuck, September 2006.

Gloria Broadcasts Her Thanks

John Reid, Kevin Hendricks, The Hagen Family, Brent Earl, Andy Northrup, Judy Lawrence, Heather. D. Swain, Ron Jenkins, The Edmonton International Fringe Theatre Festival, Klodyne Rodney, Kyle Edgar, Lou Baisi, Kim Knapp, Berend McKenzie, Anne Kupis, Michael McDonnell, James Ross, Mark Warren, Gerry Kasten, David Taylor, Ross Hahn, Shawn Bourgeault, Shelley Cornfield, Dorky-Louise, Neon, Terry Robison, Ivan Seymour, Shanann Zinger, Duane Shave, Micheale Anderson, Christopher Peterson, Rick Jessome, Con Dragu, Linda Brenneman-Snider, Brenda Knight, Gene Kosowan, Brenda O'Donnell, Ruth Smillie, Jacquie Richardson, Brad Moss, Theatre Network, Marcie Whitecotton-Carroll, Stanley Carroll, Catherine Hedlin, D. Hackman, Clifford McDowell, Ben Henderson, Kristy Harcourt, CJSR, Gaywire, First Night Festival, Memi Von Gaza, Peter Field, Henk Kalkman, Mark Bilko, Edmonton City Hall, Ian Jackson, Gina Moe, James Chipman, Gina Puntil, Robert Shannon, Janice Williamson, Robert W. Gray, Dick Finkel, Pamela Anthony, Michael Vonn, Shelley Switzer, Annie Krisher, Sean C. Wager, David Hennessey, Trevor Anderson, Patrick Monohan, Ruth Dyckfehderau, Heather Zwicker, Garrett Epp, Linda Tucker, Deb Dudek, Rebar, Brad Courtney, Kieran McKinney, Dr. Kathryn Jones, Dr. Lorne Warneke, University of Alberta, University of Regina, Grant MacEwan College, Miki Stricker, David Cheoros, James Decker, David Chimco, The Imperial Sovereign Court of the Wild Rose, Leslie Dawson, Liz Nicholls, Alan Kellogg, Dave Kelly, Tasha Bradsell, Adriana Salvia, Bridget Weiss, Norm Fassbender, Kate Holowach, Gosia Kamela, Edmonton's theatre community, the Sterling Awards, Globe Theatre, Edmonton International Street Performer's Festival, Winnipeg Fringe Festival, Little Sister's Bookstore, Greenwood's Bookshoppe, Heaven, Workshop West Theatre, Michael Clark, Shannon Paddon, Loud &

Queer Cabaret, SEE Magazine, Chapters, Buddy's Niteclub, staff and patrons of Reflections Cabaret, Café Browse, The Roost, William McDuff Gillis, The Gillis Family, Barbara McDuff, Priscilla Love, Kristyn Love, Bo and Sparky McNail, Marion Petite, Joanne Lockwood, Rob Scanlan, Shaun Simpson, Ryan Gomes, Timmy Humphrey, Jay Wells, Trudy Parsons, Kristopher Anderson, Bruce Hare, Woody Lidstone, Bette Cahill, Cathy Jones, Brad McRae, Brandt Eisner, Semi Vujcic, Dave Schmidt, Mike Fleury, Steve & Cathy Stone, the Reverend Canon David Fletcher, Dawn Sloane, Wave Magazine, the Doctors and Nurses of Victoria General Hospital & the Nova Scotia Cancer Centre, Dorothy, Friends of Dorothy, Candas Jane Dorsey and Timothy J. Anderson of The Books Collective, Ruth Linka and Diane Shaw of Brindle & Glass Publishing, every drag queen I ever met in Vancouver, Edmonton, Calgary, Regina, Saskatoon, Winnipeg, Toronto, and Halifax (and the rest I haven't met yet), anyone who has ever worked on, or come to a Guys In Disguise show . . . and everyone else.

Photo Credits

Peter McClure: cover shot, p. viii (The Burger Barn shots)

Ian Jackson: back cover, p. 144, 152, 167, 199

Richard Siemens: p. 112, 116, 120

Anne Grant: p. 122, 124, 131

Michael Brennan: dedication page, p.14, 33, 246

Ivan Seymour, artist: p. 6 (Hole Family Thanksgiving and FlashQuack)

David Williams: p. 64

Scott Melnyk: p. 154

James Shedden: p. 163

Ellie Brewer: p. 106, 110

Perry Crann, p. 162

David Taylor, p. 220. "The Supper Before Last" © used with permission.

All other photos courtesy of the Lulu Collection, the Neon Collection, the Twiggy Collection, the Ricky Collection, the Gloria Collection, and the Flashback Collection.

DARRIN HAGEN is an award-winning writer, composer, actor, and television host, as well as Canada's most notorious drag performer. In 2003, Hagen became the first Drag Queen to host a national television series, and was honoured with the Rosie Award (Alberta Motion Picture Association) for best Male Host, for "Who's On Top?" He has been awarded five Elizabeth Sterling Haynes Awards for his work in Edmonton Theatre. For his company, Guys In Disguise, specialists in cross-dressing comedy, he has created thirteen pieces of theatre that have been produced across Canada and in the US. He has become a regular speaker at universities and colleges, delivering keynote addresses at several international conferences on gender diversity. Recently Hagen was named as one of 100 Edmontonians of the Century for the city's centennial anniversary celebrations. His name came alphabetically right after Wayne Gretzky's. To the best of his knowledge, he's the only Drag Queen on that list.

PLAYS BY DARRIN HAGEN
The Edmonton Queen
Tornado Magnet: A Salute to Trailer Court Women
Tranny, Get Your Gun! (Hagen / Craddock)
Men Are Stoopid, Women Are Cra-azy (Hagen / Craddock)
PileDriver! (Hagen / Borg)
Li'l Orphan Tranny (Hagen / Craddock)
Tranne Of Green Gables (Hagen / Craddock)
The Glory, The Fury
Inventing Rasputin
BitchSlap!
Day 412
The Neo-Nancies: Hitler's Kickline
Planes, Trans and Automobiles (Hagen / Anderson)

ACKNOWLEDGEMENTS

Thanks are due to the Alberta Foundation for the Arts and to the Brenda Strathern Writing Prize for financial assistance in completing this book. *Prairie Fire* published an earlier version of "Jake" and CBC *Anthology* produced a Rebee story for CBC Radio. Thank you to the editors.

With much gratitude to everyone at NeWest Press, especially Andrew Wilmot, designer Natalie Olsen, and my wise and gentle editor, Anne Nothof. My heartfelt thanks goes to Rosemary Nixon, Aritha van Herk, Nicole Markotić, Annabel Lyon and Eunice Scarfe for their inspiration and early encouragement. Special thanks to my writing buddies, Kari Strutt, Heather Ellwood, Michael Davie, Lisa Willemse, and Cathy Jewison, for keeping me at my desk. I owe so much to my parents, Irma and Louis, my dearest sisters, Judy and Brenda, and my forever friends, Brenda and Pat.

Deepest love and gratitude to Breanna and Megan, whose tender love fills me, to Craig, for being family in all good ways, and to Jim, for being what matters most.

FRAN KIMMEL was born and raised in Calgary, Alberta. After graduating from the University of Calgary with a degree in Sociology, she worked an eclectic mix of jobs including youth worker, career counsellor, proposal writer, and a ten-year stint as a VP for a career consulting firm. Fran's stories have appeared in literary journals across Canada and have twice been nominated for the Journey Prize. Fran currently lives in Lacombe with her husband and overly enthusiastic silver Lab. This is her first novel.